ANDREW
EAMES

SOMETHING
DIFFERENT
FOR THE
WEEKEND

D1350275

WWW.BRADTGUIDES.COM
BRADT TRAVEL GUIDES LTD, UK
THE GLOBE PEQUOT PRESS INC, USA

HOME FRONT

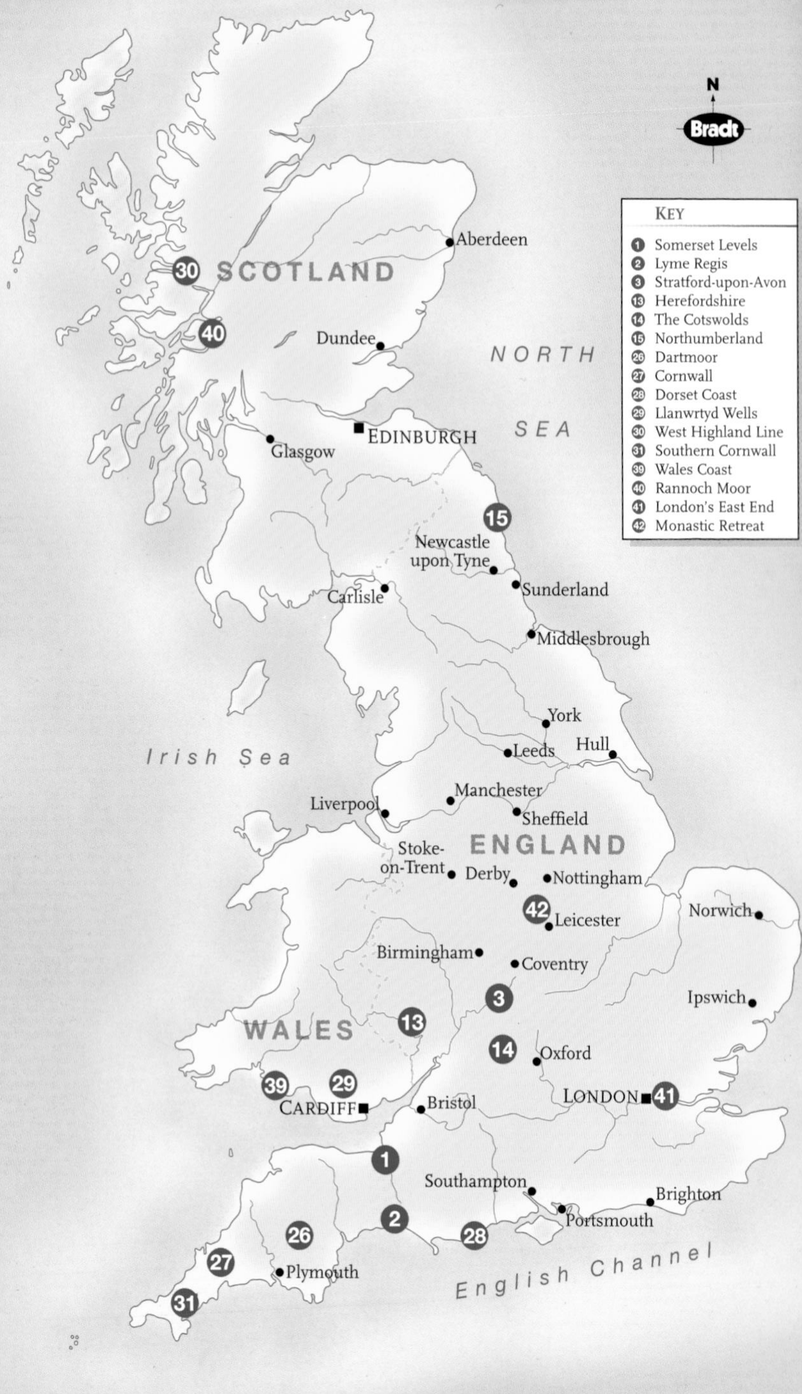

N
Bradt
KEY
1 Somerset Levels
2 Lyme Regis
3 Stratford-upon-Avon
13 Herefordshire
14 The Cotswolds
15 Northumberland
26 Dartmoor
27 Cornwall
28 Dorset Coast
29 Llanwrtyd Wells
30 West Highland Line
31 Southern Cornwall
39 Wales Coast
40 Rannoch Moor
41 London's East End
42 Monastic Retreat
SCOTLAND
Aberdeen
Dundee
NORTH SEA
EDINBURGH
Glasgow
Newcastle upon Tyne
Sunderland
Carlisle
Middlesbrough
York
Leeds
Hull
Irish Sea
Manchester
Liverpool
Sheffield
ENGLAND
Stoke-on-Trent
Derby
Nottingham
Leicester
Norwich
Birmingham
Coventry
Ipswich
WALES
Oxford
LONDON
CARDIFF
Bristol
Southampton
Brighton
Portsmouth
Plymouth
English Channel
30
40
15
42
3
13
14
39
29
41
1
2
26
28
27
31

MEDIUM DISTANT / FURTHER FLUNG

KEY

4. Vosges
5. Jokkmokk
6. The Golden Circle
7. Mont St Michel
8. Niederlausitz
9. Mallorca
10. Sahara
11. Tenerife
12. The Gambia
16. Finistère
17. Nürburgring
18. Transylvania
19. Lake Balaton
20. Ulm
21. Loire Valley
22. Lakes Bled and Bohinj
23. Red Sea
24. El Hierro
25. Lofoten islands
32. Linz
33. Niedersachsen
34. Dalsland
35. Galicia
36. Aube en Champagne
37. Hamburg
38. Aleppo
43. County Cork
44. The Wachau
45. Nice
46. Ghent
47. Ruhr Valley
48. Mini-cruising
49. San Marino
50. Nuremberg
51. Cape Breton
52. Atlas Mountains

WINTER

WINTER

SPRING

19

20

22

23
EGYPT
St Catherine's
Monastery,
home of the
burning bush.
(AE) Page 93

25
NORWAY
The Lofoten
Islands, where
the sun won't
go to bed.
(Arctic)
Page 101

Summer

Autumn

AUTHOR

Andrew Eames started his career in journalism in the Far East in the 1980s. At that stage he didn't think of himself as a travel writer, but when he returned to the UK he realised he knew a lot about a part of the world that was of great interest to the travel industry.

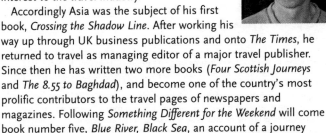

Accordingly Asia was the subject of his first book, *Crossing the Shadow Line*. After working his way up through UK business publications and onto *The Times*, he returned to travel as managing editor of a major travel publisher. Since then he has written two more books (*Four Scottish Journeys* and *The 8.55 to Baghdad*), and become one of the country's most prolific contributors to the travel pages of newspapers and magazines. Following *Something Different for the Weekend* will come book number five, *Blue River, Black Sea*, an account of a journey down the Danube, published by Transworld in autumn 2008.

AUTHOR STORY

This book was born out of frustration. Frustration with the increasingly upmarket travel sections of newspapers and magazines, obsessing about spas and designer hotels. As a traveller, I know that there are a lot of people like me out there who couldn't give a rootin-tootin hoot about designer flim-flam, but who travel for the exhilaration of the journey and the novelty and the cultural exchange in the destination.

There's a lot of that in these pages, but I'm not claiming it's easy. A real wild one like heading off into the Swedish wilderness on a rail-trolley (34 Going multi-modal in the wilderness) takes some organisation, but you might just wake up, as I did, with a browsing moose at the lakeside just outside your tent. There are other challenges, too. For the pudding club weekend (14 Custard-fest in the Cotswolds) the purpose is to eat as much spotted dick etc as possible, which sounds easier than it is. Personally I was disappointed with my performance, but I blame the custard.

When you travel for a living, as I do, you end up doing a lot of repetitive things in a lot of eminently forgettable places. These, however, are the places, and the experiences, I do remember.

First edition published January 2008

Bradt Travel Guides Ltd
23 High Street, Chalfont St Peter, Bucks SL9 9QE, England.
www.bradtguides.com
Published in the USA by The Globe Pequot Press Inc,
246 Goose Lane,
PO Box 480, Guilford, Connecticut 06475-0480

Text copyright © 2008 Andrew Eames
Maps copyright © 2008 Bradt Travel Guides Ltd
Illustrations copyright © 2008 Individual photographers and artists
Cover design by James Nunn

ISBN-10: 1 84162 209 5   ISBN-13: 978 1 84162 209 5
British Library Cataloguing in Publication Data
A catalogue record for this book is available from the British Library

Photographs www.arcticphoto.co.uk (Arctic), Brittany Ferries (BF), www.classic-
sailing.co.uk (CS), Brian O'Connell/www.mizenhead.ie (BC), Cornish Tipi Holidays
(CTH), Andrew Eames (AE), Giemme/Tips (G/Tips), Hungarian National Tourist
Office (HT), RV Jones/Pictures of Britain (RVJ), Art Kowalsky/Alamy (AK/Alamy),
www.linz.at (L), Dereck Lister Hallam/Pictures of Britain (DLH),
Photononstop/Tips (P/Tips), Preseli Venture/www.preseliventure.co.uk (PV), Andy
Sewell/Britain on View (AS), Andy Stammers/The Pudding Club (AS), Manfred
Vollmer/Landschaftspark Dusburg-Nord (MV)
Title page Sámi man, Sweden (AE), Lake Balaton (HT), Linz (L), Coasteering (PV)
Part openers Summer: Travelshots.com/Alamy, Winter: sciencephotos/Alamy,
Autumn: Andrea Jones/Alamy, Spring: Frank Blackburn/Alamy

Maps Dave Priestley   **Illustrations** Dave Colton (www.cartoonist.net)

Typeset from the author's disc by Wakewing
Printed and bound in India at Nutech Photolithographer, New Delhi

Contents

Introduction

Welcome to my personal world of wonderful and weird weekends. If you've purchased this book, congratulations; not only have you helped feed a poor starving travel writer, but you've graduated from O-level tourism to A-level travel, and you're possibly even heading for a degree.

This selection of weekends is aimed at the reader who has already done the most obvious trips to the likes of Prague, Paris and Amsterdam, and is ready to move away from the herd to root out something different. Something more distinctive and more adventurous that might stimulate a traveller's palate; something that might even challenge what constitutes a weekend break. I know you're out there, you short-haul under-grads; I've sat next to you on flights to little-known places like Balaton and Verona-Brescia, and I've seen you disappearing off into the gathering dusk with purposeful stride.

In 25 years as a travel writer I'm lucky enough to have been to a lot of places myself, but many of them didn't make the cut as far as this book is concerned. This collection centres on those which really rocked my boat; those that had the tingle factor, that changed my opinion of something, someone or somewhere. I'm fairly convinced that some of them will rock your tingle factor, too.

Of course, there's a lot of fairly self-indulgent stuff in here. No doubt a police psychologist would be able to build up a perpetrator's profile from my contents list, so let me confess to some of my peccadilloes straightaway: I love wilderness areas, I like bicycles and trains, and I think Germany is under-appreciated as a destination; I'm keen on outdoor activities, eastern Europe and the much-maligned Middle East, and I couldn't really give a monkeys for luxury resorts beloved by glossy mags and B-list celebs.

Destinations with big PR machines get more than enough coverage already in the national press to need any help from me. On the contrary, this book is my personal PR for those places which don't have the marketing muscle to elbow their way into the mainstream, places that are nevertheless aesthetically, physically, intellectually – and any other ally I can think of – up my alley, and hopefully up your alley too.

The 50 suggestions in the book constitute a year's worth of weekends, arranged into four seasons. Each season is sub-divided into *Home Front* (UK), *Medium Distant* (ie: Europe) and *Further Flung*. All are doable in two to four days, even the flashier trips to the likes of the Sahara, Nova Scotia and west Africa. Some are seasonal adventures, such as ice-driving on frozen lakes in Sweden or renting a wigwam in a converted quarry in Cornwall; some are cultural adventures like staying with a Count in Transylvania or a safari around industrial dinosaurs in Germany; and some are gastronomic experiences such as a pudding weekend in the Cotswolds or a grape-picking break in Champagne.

Aware of the environmental impact of this book's concept, I've tried to reduce the number of flights where possible by recommending trains and ships instead. But the practical detail is not intended to be comprehensive; I'm sharing the bare bones of the idea with you, and giving you a head start in organising it – the rest is up to you. You are a Bradt reader after all.

And even if you try only one of these weekends and it gives you pleasure, then I'll count this book a success.

WINTER

So Christmas is done and your goose is thoroughly cooked. Thinking of hunkering down in front of a nice warm TV until the daffodils appear? Well forget it. There's a lot of good travel to be done at this time of year; it's just a matter of using your imagination.

In the UK it's time to approach the countryside from a different perspective. Head for the Somerset Levels, where floods are part of the winter landscape; search for fossils on the shore at Lyme Regis, where winter storms will have dislodged them from the cliffs; or do Shakespeare in Stratford before all the Americans arrive. (*HOME FRONT* 1–3)

Over in Europe you can flush out your system on France's Water Route, where some of the H_2O is thicker than a consommé. In Holland, Old Masters and East Indies overlap around the Golden Circle of former trading ports on the Ijsselmeer. There's more water around Normandy's steepled Mont St Michel, which is at its most charismatic when its lanes are empty and only seabirds line the parapets. For some people, the dead of winter is a time for celebration, particularly the reindeer-herding Sámi, north of the Arctic Circle. But if you must have warmth, then seek it out in a giant hangar southeast of Berlin which was originally built for zeppelins. Or wait until March before nipping down to Mallorca to rent a bike at orange blossom time. (*MEDIUM DISTANT* 4–9)

There is some serious sun available if you're prepared to travel (and to pay), with dry heat courtesy of the Sahara Desert right in the south of Tunisia, and damper, tropical heat courtesy of Gambia, west Africa, where you could spend your days in a dugout canoe, drinking palm wine. And then there's good old Tenerife, but I'm suggesting you try a corner of the tourist-infested island that not many people know. (*FURTHER FLUNG* 10–12)

PRICE GRADING FOR ACCOMMODATION

$ – up to £40 for a double room; $$ – £40–70 double; $$$ – £70–110 double; $$$$ – £110 + double.

DESTINATIONS

HOME FRONT

MEDIUM DISTANT

FURTHER FLUNG

Welly weather in the Somerset Levels

1

WINTER FLOODS TRANSFORM THE SOMERSET LEVELS,
ISOLATING RUINED ISLAND MONASTERIES AND THE
HUMP WHERE KING ALFRED BURNT THE CAKES.
ARTISTS LIVE AND WORK HERE, SCATTERED ALONG A
RIVERSIDE TRAIL THAT WINDS THROUGH THE LEVELS.

MIDWINTER RAIN DOESN'T USUALLY BRING OUT THE
best in the Great British Countryside, but there
is one part of this land where over-brimming
rivers are a fact of life and where endless
precipitation doesn't equate to frustrated noses
pressed against the windowpane.

The onset of winter may bring peoplessness to our
mountains and render our woodlands leafless and drab,
but in the Somerset Levels it heralds a makeover that
fills the lowering skies with flickering life and draws
great bedsheets of water up around villages of honey-
coloured limestone.

These sheets of white are stitched by marching
rows of pollarded willows, decorated with coots, herons and
migratory wetland birds, and threaded by raised dykes bearing
walkers in wellies. This is the time of year when the locals park their
vehicles on high ground and resort to tractors for the school run.

The Levels are essentially the peaty floodplains of the rivers
Parrett, Huntspill, Brue and the King's Sedgemoor Drain. The whole
area was once a semi-permanent inland sea stretching all the way
from Yeovil to the Bristol Channel and inhabited only by eel hunters
who lived in villages built on stilts. It was eventually drained in the
13th century by rich and powerful abbots on their own little islands
at Glastonbury, Muchelney and Athelney, after they got fed up with
being cut off every winter.

SOMERSET
LEVELS

Today, the landscape is at its most distinctive along the banks of the river Parrett around Langport. Here Muchelney Abbey may be in ruins but its setting is still essentially medieval, and still isolated by winter floods. Nearby Athelney, where King Alfred supposedly made a hash of his buns, is today just a grassy mound, but Burrow Mump, another medieval church-topped island, rises out of the winter water as it has always done.

All are within walking distance of each other down the Parrett Trail, which runs along high dykes past rhynes, sluice gates and pumping stations. The Trail runs all the way from source to estuary, a distance of around 50 miles, and has been studded with stiles, seats and bridges specially made by local artists.

This has long been a place of creativity. The current stable of artists includes John Leach, a jolly, shaggy figure who has been fashioning blushing pots at Muchelney Pottery for 40 years. Just down the road at Stoke St Gregory, site of the Willows and Wetland Centre, Serena de la Hey bends the Levels' most traditional crop to her will, making geese, swans and running dogs out of willow. Her most famous creation is the *Running Man*, a huge willow giant alongside the M5 motorway just north of Bridgwater, welcoming visitors to the southwest.

Eating and drinking is done differently here, too. Martock's Bakery Royal produces a lardy cake that the old gentlemen dip in sherry to sustain them through the winter. Then there's the Burrow Hill Cider Farm at Kingsbury Episcopi, a unique institution with huge barrels, rootling chickens and piles of musty apples, like a scene straight out of Thomas Hardy. This is the first cider brandy distillery in recorded history to be granted a licence by HM Customs, and its Somerset Royal is stocked by the likes of Harvey Nichols and Fortnum & Mason for a huge price, not really justified by the taste.

Much more rewarding is Burrow Hill's crisp, dry cider, available at most of the local hostelries, including the Wyndham Arms at Kingsbury Episcopi, also on the Parrett Trail. The Wyndham's menu is based on homemade pies and it has an open log fire ideal for walkers' toes – plus a pub kitten which interprets the emergence of stockinged toes as a declaration of war.

The Levels' free-thinkers tend to gather at the Halfway House at Pitney, an unreconstructed flagstoned pub with huge pine tables and copies of *The Spectator*, *Private Eye* and that day's newspapers, helped down by cider, ale from the cask and a choice of six different homemade curries, including Jamaican curried goat.

But the most idiosyncratic of all the local drinking places has to be the Rose and Crown in Huish Episcopi, still known to locals as 'Eli's Place' after the man who used to be the landlord here 50 years ago. Eli's Place is now run by Eli's grandson and granddaughters, but without the assistance of an actual bar; the hand pumps are set against the walls and regulars help themselves and are relied on to put the right money in the wooden drawer. There is still table service in The Men's Kitchen, the back room is reserved for Spoofing, a traditional drinking game of betting on coins, and one old farmer still sells his vegetables in the front room every Saturday morning.

The Rose and Crown is far too much of a throwback to ever win a pub of the year competition, but it is a symbol of a community that likes to do things its own way, never mind the rain.

PRACTICALITIES

GETTING THERE

The Somerset Levels sit between Wells, Glastonbury and the sea, accessible from the M5 junction 23.

TOURIST INFORMATION

Bow Street, Langport (☎ 01458 253527)
A detailed **Parrett Trail guide** is available at most tourist offices, or by writing to Yeovil Visitor Information Centre, Hendford, Yeovil, Somerset BA20 1UN (☎ 01935 845946; *www.somerset.gov.uk/somerset/ete/rpt*). Price £5.95.

CYCLE HIRE

Being flat, this is excellent cycling country.
Bow Bridge Cycles
☎ 01458 250350
Has bikes and a variety of route suggestions.

ACCOMMODATION

Muchelney Ham Farm $ $
☎ 01458 250737; *www.muchelneyhamfarm.co.uk*
Excellent B&B in an immaculate 17th-century farmhouse.
Farthings Hotel $ $ $ $
Hatch Beauchamp
☎ 01823 480664; *www.farthingshotel.co.uk*
This is more formal; ask for the room which has its en-suite bathroom up a spiral staircase.

PLACES OF INTEREST

Burrow Hill Cider Farm
☎ 01460 240782; *www.ciderbrandy.co.uk*
Kingsbury Episcopi
Rose and Crown
Huish Episcopi
☎ 01458 250494

LYME REGIS'S OLD FOSSILS

FOSSIL HUNTING ALONG THE SHORE IN THE DORSET
RESORT WHICH WAS THE SETTING FOR THE *FRENCH
LIEUTENANT'S WOMAN*. WINTER STORMS MAKE THE
CLIFFS AND BEACH AT LYME PRIME FOSSIL TERRITORY,
AND THIS WEEKEND IS MADE ALL THE MORE
INTERESTING BY ECCENTRIC ACCOMMODATION AND A
WALK WHICH CAN BE TOO TOLKEINESQUE FOR
COMFORT.

LYME REGIS WORKS WELL OUT OF SEASON. WEDGED
into a scalloped cleft in swirling hills that
supposedly inspired Tolkein's vision of Hobbit-
land, it is a maze of a place which is variously
smugglers' port, elegant Georgian spa, and 1950s'
bucket-and-spade resort. Its 16th-century scramble
of lanes, tipped down to the seafront, were never
designed for summer traffic.

Lyme is a place of stories, long associated with
artists and writers, where Jane Austen once took her
holidays. Art shops, bookshops and fine food shops
still dominate the steep main street, which has yet
to succumb to the likes of Next, Dixons or Greggs.
Look out particularly for Chimp and Zee, an Aladdin's Cave of
children's literature by resident writers Catherine and Laurence
Anholt, Lyme's successors to John Fowles, the town's reclusive
literary giant until his recent death.

Down by the shore, the town's seafront terraces are like defensive
castellations; the ancient jetty, the Cobb, a giant apostrophe of stone
that curls out from the shore, but not quite immense enough to
stop the winter waves from flopping their forelocks over the outer

wall. The furthest point is where Meryl Streep famously lingered in the film version of Fowles's *French Lieutenant's Woman*, getting a gentle hosing from the salty spray.

If you haven't seen the film you might be able to pick up a DVD from Bob Speer in the Sanctuary Bookshop, down by the sea. Bob, usually in a Tilley hat and sometimes assisted by his Japanese wife Mariko, is one of Lyme's eccentrics. He usually has a couple of restored pianolas in store, and will occasionally sit down at one or other to pump out jazz. He has original Beryl Cook illustrations in the window, a collection of Miles Kington books on the mantelshelf for the benefit of all customers, and will point out the best bits from the little-known classic *Lady Loverly's Chatter*. The man plainly can't resist books in any shape or form, and if you decide to stay in his booklovers' bed and breakfast, in rooms above the shop, you'll be sharing the staircase, the bedroom, the bathroom and the breakfast room with yet more of his collection. You might find yourself eating your breakfast (Japanese menu if you wish) staring at the spine of a history of orgies with the title *Flagellation and the Flagellantes*.

Bob Speer's original intention was to create an environment in which people would come to write their own books in the rooms above his shop, but in reality many more of Lyme's winter visitors are treasure-hunters who spread out along the shore, for Lyme is the pivotal point of the UNESCO World Heritage Site-listed Jurassic Coast.

If you want a dinosaur named after you, then this is both the right place and the right time to find one. Winter storms pound at the shore cliffs both here and at neighbouring Charmouth, keeping half-a-dozen professional fossil hunters well occupied.

For amateurs, there are regular guided fossil walks to show you what's what. These are advertised all over town, outside Lyme's small seafront museum, and in front of the private Dinosaurland museum. Geologists are not normally known for their small talk, although Dinosaurland's softly spoken Steve Davies, who gave up a highly remunerative career with BP to settle here, is a particularly interesting one. Under their guidance you are bound to find bullet-shaped belemnites by the dozen, delicate ammonites in fool's gold the size of 10p pieces, and ichthyosaurus bones. If you don't find anything, the guides will help you out with something they found earlier.

The whole business of making money out of these fossils is slightly controversial, because theoretically everything that falls onto the foreshore belongs to the Crown, and therefore can't be sold by an individual who just picks it up. Academic institutions get riled when finds are sold overseas. But if they weren't picked up they'd be destroyed by the sea. The business has its own internal problems, too, with a couple of the local professionals having a problem with theft – theft based on obvious insider knowledge.

One of those professionals is Chris Moore, who has a workshop called Forge Fossils in nearby Charmouth. Moore, a self-effacing Mancunian, has found two new species of ichthyosaurus (marine reptiles), one of which is named after him. His workshop has curiosities like fossilised shark poo and a perfectly preserved dragonfly which had been trapped in a mud slide 190 million years ago.

But whether you're professional or amateur, your fossil hunting will be governed by the wind, the rain and particularly the tides. High water will inevitably prevent you adopting the quarter-past-six position on the beach, britches to the breeze. This is the moment to climb up into the region known as the Undercliff, for the walk that supposedly inspired Tolkein.

Despite its name, the Undercliff actually runs along the top of the cliffs, along a section where centuries of landslips have created an other-worldly tangle of vegetation and mossy shadows. The South West Coast Path runs for several miles towards Seaton through this difficult terrain. It is unusual and atmospheric, but not really the place for a long winter walk on your own.

LYME REGIS'S OLD FOSSILS

PRACTICALITIES

GETTING THERE

Lyme is 26 miles east of Exeter along the A3052. The nearest rail station (*www.nationalrail.co.uk*) is Axminster, where a local bus meets every train.

TOURIST INFORMATION

Lyme Regis (☎ *01297 442138*) and more general regional information on the Jurassic Coast (*www.jurassiccoast.com*).

ACCOMMODATION

Bob and Mariko Speer's Booklovers B&B §
Above the Sanctuary Bookshop, Broad Street
☎ *01297 445815; www.lyme-regis.demon.co.uk*
Eccentric but well appointed.

Hotel Alexandra § § §
Up the hill on Pound Street
☎ *01297 442010; www.hotelalexandra.co.uk*
Traditionally elegant with great views and a big lawn, this hotel has been run by the same family for 29 years.

PLACES OF INTEREST

Dinosaurland
☎ *01297 443541; www.dinosaurland.co.uk*
Forge Fossils
☎ *01297 560005*

3

STRATFORD-UPON-AVON
WITHOUT YOUR GRAN

IN A BOOK OF ECCENTRICS, DOING SHAKESPEARE IN
STRATFORD MIGHT SEEM RATHER AN OBVIOUS THING
TO DO – BUT IT IS SO QUINTESSENTIALLY ENGLISH
THAT WE TEND TO LEAVE IT TO THE AMERICANS. AND
DON'T BE PUT OFF BY 'THE BARD'S' RATHER PRISSY,
NATIONAL TREASURE STATUS IN HIS HOME TOWN. IT'S
ONLY SKIN DEEP.

IF, LIKE ME, YOU HADN'T BEEN TO STRATFORD SINCE
your granny took you there as an adolescent, it
is high time you gave it another chance.

Of course, there's oodles of whimsy all over
Stratford, which has a rather saccharine Shakes-
industry that starts the moment you roll in across
its 15th-century bridge. 'Please park prettily', reads
the sign in the car park of the eminently atmospheric
Shakespeare Hotel, where every room is named
after a Shakespearean character. But frankly, it is not
easy to sashay in a Skoda.

**STRATFORD-
-UPON-AVON**

However there's no denying the visual appeal of
the town. Stratford, which is laid out in a medieval
grid, is composed of Regency terraces and half-timbered Tudor and
Elizabethan inns and tea houses. The swan-covered Avon runs
through it, and at no point in the town are you ever more than 20
yards from a toasted teacake, a pot of Earl Grey, a pint of ale, an
open fire with a stack of house newspapers, or the chance to buy a
set of Macbeth fingerpuppets.

Of all the significant Shakespeare buildings, Shakespeare
Birthplace – a rambling half-timbered house in the heart of town – is
the most authentic, and you can't really avoid going round it. Mind
you, not all the detailing seems quite right; my eye was caught by

the sort of screen from behind which you'd normally expect to hear someone shouting 'nurse, nurse!' followed by unpleasant gurglings. Here you'll learn how Will's dad was a bit of a lad, refusing to attend church and being fined for a 'muckhill' outside his house. And there's an intimation that his son wasn't entirely the golden boy the Stratford Shakes-industry would like him to be, either, with a revealing facsimile of the great man's will in the Birthplace's museum. In it, he leaves practically nothing to his supposedly beloved wife, Anne.

Outside, there are some discordant notes too amongst the teddy-bear shops and the Laura Ashley, principally in the form of ugly blocks of 1960s' red brick. One of the odder presences is Ragdoll TV's Teletubby headquarters, across the road from the Shakespeare Hotel.

No, not everything in Stratford is stuffed, cuddly or served with jam, and that includes the plays. The main event of your visit will presumably be a production in one of the three RSC venues – the Royal Shakespeare Theatre by the riverside, or its subsidiaries the Swan Theatre or the Courtyard Theatre. Bear in mind that the RSC is a creative company, and it can't resist the temptation to re-invent and re-interpret even the old favourites, sometimes to an extent which disappoints those grannies who've dragged their grandchildren away from their games consoles for an educational matinée. Even *A Midsummer Night's Dream* can easily turn out to be a pretty dark piece, with the lost-in-the-woods leading ladies down to their bra and panties by the end of the first act. Granny isn't sitting quite so comfortably now.

For anyone interested in pursuing a more mortal image of the playwright, there's a good walking tour led by Roman-nosed actor Jonathan Milton which focuses on 'all you ever wanted to know about Shakespeare but were afraid to ask'. It starts from the front of the Swan Theatre and then, after a eulogy on the importance of beer in the strolling player's life, marches off into town past 'the only 16th-century Pizza Hut in Christendom'.

In typical actorly fashion Milton is happy to demolish the more prissy Shakes-myths. Ripe for a side-swipe, for example, is Anne Hathaway's cottage in the neighbouring village of Shottery, where the staff lovingly show visitors the romantic fireside bench where the peerless playwright had supposedly asked his beautiful future wife to marry him... all stuff and nonsense, according to Milton. At the time Shakespeare was 18, and Anne Hathaway was 26 – already on the shelf by the standards of the day. But he'd put a bun in her oven, so what else were they supposed to do?

Of course, we may all know a lot more about Anne Hathaway by the time this book is starting to circulate; Germaine Greer's biography is due out in autumn 2007, and no doubt dour Anne will become a much livelier character in her hands.

As Shakespeare's theatrical career started to accelerate he effectively moved away from Stratford altogether, leaving Anne Hathaway behind. In fact he only really returned on his death, and by then he certainly wasn't inclined to conform. His tomb in Holy Trinity Church, right by the altar, is guarded by his own pagan imprecation – 'curst be he who moves my bones' – to prevent anyone from digging him up. We don't exactly know what he had in mind when he used these words, but some commentators have suggested that he might not have wanted to share his afterlife with wife Anne, who would normally have had her bones buried next to his.

And then of course there's the matter of his genetics; maybe he didn't want anyone getting at his DNA to extract the Shakespeare gene. Otherwise we'd all want to buy it off the shelf like Viagra and incorporate it in our children, to be stuck in a world of rhyming couplets.

PRACTICALITIES

GETTING THERE

Stratford is rail-connected to London and Birmingham (*www.nationalrail.co.uk*), and six miles southwest of the M40 at Junction 15.

TOURIST INFORMATION

❨ *08701 607930; www.shakespeare-country.co.uk*

ACCOMMODATION

Macdonald Shakespeare Hotel $ $ $–$ $ $ $
Chapel Street, in the centre of town
❨ *0870 830 4812; www.theshakespeare-hotel.co.uk*
RSC Short Breaks
❨ *0870 043 7637; www.rscshortbreaks.co.uk*
Offers a good deal that combines hotel accommodation with RSC performances.

THEATRE

Royal Shakespeare Company
Ticket hotline ❨ *0870 609 1110; www.rsc.org.uk*
Daytime and evening performances. Ticket prices range from £5 to £42.
Theatre walks
Depart Sat 10.00; tickets from RSC box office.
Shakespeare's Birthplace and Exhibition
Henley Street
❨ *01789 204016; www.shakespeare.org.uk*
Ragdoll Productions Ltd
Opposite the Shakespeare Hotel, Chapel Street
❨ *01789 404100; www.ragdoll.co.uk*

PLACES OF INTEREST

Holy Trinity Church
❨ *01789 266316; www.stratford-upon-avon.org*

SLOSHED IN THE VOSGES

4

A POST-CHRISTMAS DETOX ON A TRADITIONAL SPA
CIRCUIT IN THE VOSGES MOUNTAINS, HOPING THAT
MINERAL WATER WILL FLUSH OUT THOSE ILL-GOTTEN
DISEASES. PERSONALLY, MY ETHOS IS THAT IF IT
DOESN'T HURT, ISN'T COLD, AND DOESN'T TAKE PLACE
EARLY IN THE MORNING, THEN IT CAN'T BE DOING
ANY GOOD, BUT THE FRENCH COME HERE ON
DOCTOR'S ORDERS.

YOU MAY THINK THAT WINE IS FRANCE'S BIGGEST-selling drink, but you'd be wrong by a country mile. Mineral water is huge business in Europe's gourmet nation, at least in terms of volume sold. At the last count there were 1,200 varieties of bottled water in the shops, each with its own particular characteristic, although that characteristic often gets lost in translation in the UK. Did you know, for example, that Evian is best for babies, and Vichy for gout? Well now you do.

THE VOSGES

Anyway two of the top sellers, Vittel and Contrex, have their source in the Vosges Mountains, although the word 'mountains' rather over-glorifies this rolling, forested landscape 200 miles to the southeast of Paris. And if you don't want to just drink the stuff, two more traditional spa towns along the Water Route offer everything from *vaporisation anale* to *drainage Lymphatique*. Not forgetting *goutte à goutte rectal*. Tantalising stuff, *n'est-ce pas?*

Vittel is the big-business end of the route. The promo material suggests the town is full of floppy-haired blondes, bounding in slo-mo across the grass (but with little in the way of bouncy bits). The reality, of course, is otherwise. The fluffiest grass is not for walking on, and most of the (faux) blondes have bouncy bits which it is prudent to ignore.

But there's no denying that Vittel has had a hugely invigorating effect on its environment, if not on the people within it. The immaculate centre is full of château hotels and imposing private houses, and the elegantly colonnaded spa itself was designed by the same Charles Garnier who created the Paris Opera House. The surrounding countryside is a healthy verdure of golf courses and carefully tended woodland, and all because of the water economy. Indeed, brand owners Nestlé have been busily buying up more land to ensure that no pollutants sully the sources.

There are, confusingly, three varieties of Vittel: Grand Source is for the kidney stones (drink six litres a day for three weeks to flush 'em out); Bon Source is used externally in various spa treatments; and Hépar is richly mineralled (smooth, heady, with a slight gooseberry nose). Apparently Hépar is effective against stress-related ailments.

Contrex is also a big brand in France, perhaps because it sounds like something used to clean contact lenses. Its home, Contrexéville, lies just 6km to the southwest of Vittel. Opened back in 1774 and much patronised by Napoleon III, it's a bit more aristocratic than Vittel, and a touch more discreet, partly because of its profile as 'the slimmers' spa'.

Most people come here on prescribed plans which incorporate exercise, spa treatments, and food and water intake into an overall slimmers' package, the Forfait Minceur. The hotels have special three-course *menus du jour* with a calorie content no greater than a Mars bar. And if you feel hungry, then you head down to the glass-walled *rotonde* and get on the outside of a few more sulphurous-smelling glasses of raw Contrex.

Apparently an increasing number of men are going on Contrex cures, perhaps because of Contrex's 'four-hand' massage. The latter is the massage equivalent of synchronised swimming, administered by that awesome trinity, Sandrine and Pascaline with the Vaseline. In this case the 'under water' means lying under parallel sprinklers squirting Contrex, while these two belles in bathing suits do the business. Frankly, not very relaxing at all.

From Contrexéville, the Water Route lopes southeast across gentle hills, crosses the Canal de L'Est, and pauses briefly in Bains les Bains. This is how French spas used to be: slightly old and sad. The Bains les Bains clients are true *curistes* and are largely funded by the state, whereas Vittel and Contrex get most of their business from private individuals. Once upon a time France's 108 spas were all state funded like this, and catered to colonial officers and soldiers purging their systems. Today, with more antibiotics and tighter purse strings, the – pardon me – bottom is falling out of that traditional market, and Bains les Bains is suffering.

Happily the last spa on this route, Plombières les Bains, is in far better shape. Its Art-Deco *rotonde* has the feeling of easily familiarity, of a meeting point of the same folks year after year.

Plombières is composed of a trellis of alleys, railings and wrought-iron balconies wedged into a deep fissure of a valley about 50 miles southeast of Vittel. In the space of 100 yards there are 27 different springs in the valley bottom, some of them up to 80°C. None of them is bottled, but each is supposed to have a slightly different curative property ranging from the spine (Source Alliot) to the eyes (Source Sainte Claire).

They've been around a long time. Romans used to lounge around in mineral-water *piscines* here, and today's treatments are still housed in the original spa buildings: the underground galleries date from Roman times, and the rest of it from the era when Louis XV, Napoleon III and consumptive authors hung out here in the hope that the water might flush away their disreputable diseases.

But the nice thing about Plombières is that the renovated spa – Calodae – is charmingly amateurish compared with the big-business venues of Vittel and Contrexéville. Accordingly, it's full of novices like myself, wandering around the corridors, peering into cubicles, smelling like a high tide, and being squirted at from all ends.

PRACTICALITIES

GETTING THERE

Vittel is five hours by train from Paris (*www.sncf.com*), but in order to travel from one spa to the next you're going to need a car, or even a bicycle (can be hired in Vittel). The Water Route (Route Thermale) is clearly marked with blue signs.

TOURIST INFORMATION

The website *www.vosges.fr/cg88/testoffice/document.asp?num=70&lan=2* has links to all the spas.

ACCOMMODATION

Club Med
➤ *08453 676767; www.clubmed.co.uk*
Club Med have a big presence in Vittel, but tend to base their stays on week-long packages.

Plombières les Bains $–$ $
➤ *+33 29 30 07 07; www.plombieres-les-bains.com*
More geared to day or weekend visitors, and you can get inexpensive accommodation in one of their purpose-built hotels (have a look at the website) with various treatments included.

5

REINDEER-FANCYING IN JOKKMOKK

FORGET THE ICEHOTEL OR GOING TO SEE FATHER
CHRISTMAS IN LAPLAND. THE GENUINE WINTER
DESTINATION HEREABOUTS IS THE SÁMI FESTIVAL AT
JOKKMOKK, NORTHERN SWEDEN, WHERE YOU CAN
LEARN 1,000 DIFFERENT THINGS TO DO WITH
REINDEER, DEAD OR ALIVE. WITH TEMPERATURES
WELL BELOW FREEZING, IT MAY BE ADVISABLE TO
HAVE ICE-DRIVING LESSONS WHEN YOU ARRIVE.

FOR A CULTURAL CAPITAL, JOKKMOKK DOESN'T LOOK
like much. But this unremarkable crossroads
town in the far north of Sweden – more northerly
than the Arctic Circle – is actually the spiritual
centre of the colourful, nomadic Sámi or Lapp
people, who live right across the northern
regions of Norway, Sweden and Finland.

Jokkmokk started life as winter quarters
for reindeer herders, but today it is the
meeting place for the multi-national Sámi
parliamentary assembly, a sort of government without power which
has representatives from Sámi people from all over northern
Scandinavia. Jokkmokk also has the Sámi library, and has the only
college in the country which teaches reindeer husbandry in the Sámi
language, a *very* vocational course. But for much of the year the
town slumbers, because the Sámi themselves are away in their
summer camps, way away across the tundra.

Come to Sámi territory in midsummer, and you can travel around
on the charismatic old *Inlandsbanan*, with a stop at Jokkmokk
station. The stop is ostensibly to visit the so-called 'Mosquito
Museum', but the station is just a platform parked on a bit of bog,

with no roads or houses visible; in fact it's a rather lugubrious Scandinavian joke. The 'museum' is just a façade; open the door and there is just more bog, forest and tundra on the other side... and mosquitoes the size of jump-jets for whom the opening of the door means only one thing: lunch. The best thing that can be said about mozzies is that they are compassionate creatures; kill one, and several hundred arrive for the funeral. Needless to say, most passengers retreat swiftly to the train.

Sámi territory in winter is a completely different story. The mozzies, of course, absent themselves when it is 25 degrees below. Their place is taken by reindeer, especially in Jokkmokk in the first weekend in February. I dare say no other world capital can lay claim to as many reindeer in the main street – dead or alive. The annual winter market has come to town.

In the absence of the *Inlandsbanan*, you'll have to hire a car, probably from Luleå, the main town in the Norbotten region. Luleå has an airport and is served by a very efficient overnight sleeper (with en-suite bathroom) which even picks up from Stockholm Airport. No 'wrong kind of snow' excuses here; the whole landscape is up to its neck in the stuff, so everyone just gets on with it.

Before heading north, you can practise doing handbrake wheelies on a frozen lake like a middle-aged carjacker, which besides being cracking good fun, actually provides handy experience of how to regain control in a slide. The organisers at Ebbenjarka camp – where there's a giant Sámi wigwam – can also put together icebreaker trips, or get you to complete a Norbotten Baccalaureate (dog sledging, curling, ice driving, snowmobiling, sauna and dinner) all in a single day.

With the confidence of all that behind you, embark on the empty roads towards Jokkmokk. It is a pleasure to travel to a snowy country which isn't all mountains and melted cheese. The towns of Luleå and Piteå both have pretty little 'church villages' dating back to an era when church attendance was obligatory and travel so arduous that outlying farmers had to build themselves small wooden cottages around the church to stay over on a Saturday night.

In the countryside, the silhouettes of wooden barns mark the location of the summer fields, and the wooden houses all have that storybook, Pippi Longstocking look – all of them either painted yellow or red and each with a candle flickering in every lace-fringed window.

Jokkmokk's market, however, is less of a fairytale, and more of an anti-fur campaigner's worst nightmare. A long thread of stalls through the town centre, it is thronged with beings with rheumy faces who seem half human and half beast, so extensively are they dressed in animal skins. Many have little kick-sledges on which they coast gently through the crowds.

Occasionally this sea of people parts to allow a reindeer train through, with straining hooves, bulging eyes and a very musty smell. The deer are led by an old gent who is the spitting image of Father Christmas and followed by a procession of self-conscious children in brightly coloured Sámi beaded costumes. In fields nearby you can ride in a reindeer-hauled sleigh, gamble a few krona on racing reindeer and queue up for Sámi stew (guess which flavour) in a Sámi reindeer-skin tent.

As for the stalls, they were groaning with the sort of stuff you're unlikely to be giving your loved ones next Christmas; winsome handmade wooden skis, avalanches of knobbly handmade socks, trays of bone-handled hunting knives, shed loads of stuffed arctic foxes, and reindeer, in all stages of life and death.

On my visit, I approached one stall piled high with carcasses and skins with the intention of buying a steak for the folks at home, but the stallholder looked puzzled when I asked whether he had anything fresh. I later realised what a stupid question it had been; the air temperature was, after all, minus 25, and in those conditions the only meat that wasn't frozen was still running around.

PRACTICALITIES

GETTING THERE

SAS (☎ *0870 6072 7727; www.flysas.com*) flies from London to Stockholm and then to Luleå every day. Expect to pay upwards of £250 return. Alternatively, the Stockholm to Luleå sleeper train is run by **Connex** (☎ *+46 771 260 000; www.connex.se*). A return berth costs from £90.

TOURIST INFORMATION

Jokkmokk
☎ *+46 971 222 50; www.turism.jokkmokk.se*

TOUR OPERATOR

If you prefer a tour operator to make all your arrangements, **Arctic Experience** (☎ *0870 060 3288; www.arctic-experience.co.uk*) specialises in the area.

ACCOMMODATION

Quality Hotel $ $ $
Luleå
☎ *+46 920 201 000; www.choicehotels.se/hotels/se53*
Good facilities, in the centre of town.

Camp Ebbenjarka
☎ *+46 920 753 30; www.incoming-nordkalotten.com*
15 minutes out of Luleå, it tends to deal with group travel, but will also host individuals. Prices on application.

PLACES OF INTEREST

Sámi market
www.jokkmokksmarknad.com

THE EAST INDIES IN
A GOLDEN CIRCLE

6

THE GOLDEN CIRCLE IS A COLLECTION OF
IMMACULATE EAST INDIAN TRADING TOWNS –
HOORN, ENKHUIZEN AND EDAM – IN DUTCH POLDER
COUNTRY ON THE SHORES OF THE IJSSELMEER. A
PLACE FOR COSY HOTELS, SEAFARING HISTORY AND
WINTER WALKS.

GETTING ALL COSY AND CULTURAL IS NOT JUST THE
monopoly of cities like Paris and Brussels.
There's an area just north of Amsterdam where
the slanting wintry sunshine comes in at a
perfect trajectory for lighting up gabled
merchants' houses and etching full-bellied
sailing barges against the sky.

THE GOLDEN
CIRCLE

This is what the Dutch call the Golden
Circle, a russet-coloured region striped
with land, water and handsome towns
which could have stepped straight out of a painting by Rembrandt
or Vermeer. The dominant landscape is composed of polders, very
low, flat land largely reclaimed from the sea, protected by dykes and
laced with drainage ditches. Once upon a time there'd have been
windmills everywhere too, to keep the water moving, but these days
electric pumping stations maintain the status quo.

The big watery influence hereabouts is the giant Ijsselmeer,
formerly the Zuyder Zee, which sounds like the chorus of a
Somerset drinking song, but which was once part of the North Sea.
The handsome historic towns are Enkhuizen, Hoorn and Edam,
once noble fishing and trading ports, each within 15 minutes' drive
of the other.

Two of these three – Enkhuizen and Hoorn – are former bases for
the Dutch East India Company, which between 1602 and 1798 was

M E D I U M   D I S T A N T   **23**

the largest commercial enterprise in the world. For a century ships returned here laden with spices from what is now Indonesia, making their owners very rich in the process. As a result the towns are stuffed with immaculate merchants' homes from Holland's Golden Age, drawn up in rows by the water's edge, gabled and pointed like ballerinas.

The Zuyder Zee has long since been dammed and re-christened the Ijsselmeer after high tides regularly exasperated the locals by filling their houses with salt water. Nevertheless these fossilised ports are still crowded with the tangled rigging and polished mahogany of sailing barges.

Edam may be the Golden Circle's most famous name, but it is actually a sleepy, cobbled little place, built on a web of canals that eventually proved too narrow to sustain its 33 shipyards. Much of the old town is 17th century, and surprisingly intact and unbullied by suburbs, despite being only 15 miles from Amsterdam. There is, of course, a cheese merchant or two, but the main cheesy feature is a market in the summer months only. Instead, the real curiosity here is the Edam Museum, a 16th-century house with a bizarre floating cellar, which rises and falls with the water table and rocks like a boat when you step into it.

Edam also has one of the Golden Circle's nicest hotels, the family-run Fortuna, most of whose 24 rooms are in a clutch of cottages around a very pretty courtyard on a canal bank. The restaurant and reception are in three conjoined gabled townhouses, jammed with mirrors, paintings, cut glass and polished wood.

Edam feels pretty much unchanged, but recent years have turned Hoorn, the next place of any size to the north, into a substantial town. Nevertheless down towards the waterside the merchants' houses begin again, and the period feel returns. Of the 400 sailing barges still on the Ijsselmeer, a fair number will be moored here, surrounded by gabled façades and under the watchful eye of the 16th-century Hoofdtoren, a defensive tower at the harbour entrance which has a café upstairs.

Many of the sailing barges are charter boats and you can book passages of up to a week around the Ijsselmeer. Still, that's a pretty poor effort compared to where they used to go from here. Hoorn mariner Abel Tasman was the first to reach Tasmania; Jan Pietersz

Coen founded the Dutch trading post of Batavia (now Jakarta) and Willem Schouten named Cape Horn after his home town.

The Hoorn harbourside is where you are most likely to clamp eyes on a local fisherman, complete with clogs and braces and looking like someone out of central casting, stomping across to his net store. The traditional catch of these fishermen, herring, has long since been replaced by pike and eel now that the Ijsselmeer is no longer connected to the sea.

However herring is still on the menu in the wonderfully authentic Zuyder Zee Museum, in neighbouring Enkhuizen, once Holland's foremost herring port. The museum is in two parts, and it is in the open-air section – a gem of a preserved village – that you won't be able to miss the smell and the plume of smoke coming from the fish smokery. Sit and dissect a freshly smoked herring with your fingers, and then adjourn to the old-style café for a typical pancake slathered in cream and berries.

The indoor part of the museum, a short distance away in the harbour area of town, has a large collection of historic boats and state-of-the-art displays about the Dutch East India Company. It also tells the compelling story of the eventual damming of the Zuyder Zee.

Outside, coots and herons stalk the downtown canals. With the smell of herring lingering on your fingers, and the sight of a handful of masts in the distance, you could be forgiven for thinking that nothing had changed here at all.

PRACTICALITIES

GETTING THERE

Stena Line (☎ *0870 570 7070; www.stenaline.com*) operates the crossing between Harwich and Hook of Holland, from where Hoorn is a two-hour drive. From £140 return with car.

Hoorn and Enkhuizen both have direct rail links (*www.ns.nl*) to Amsterdam. Edam is a half-hour bus ride from directly outside Amsterdam's central station.

TOURIST INFORMATION

www.holland.com/goudencirkel

ACCOMMODATION

Hotel Fortuna $ $
Edam
☎ *+31 299 371 671; www.fortuna-edam.nl*

PLACES OF INTEREST

Zuyder Zee Museum
Enkhuizen
www.zuiderzeemuseum.nl

7

Marooned on Mont St Michel

HOLE UP ON THE MONT FOR A WINTER WEEKEND. FOR
MOST OF THE YEAR THE NARROW LANES OF THIS 11TH-
CENTURY GOTHIC MASTERPIECE ARE GUMMED SOLID
WITH TOURISTS. FAR BETTER TO COME WHEN THE RAIN
HOWLS AROUND ITS MONASTIC WALLS AND TOURISTS
ARE OUTNUMBERED BY SEABIRDS SEEKING SHELTER.

FROM A DISTANCE IT LOOKS LIKE SOMETHING OUT OF
Disney meets the *Da Vinci Code*, or perhaps the
product of a Bavarian woodcarver's over-romantic
imagination: a salvo of spires rising out of a
barnacle of rock washed up on a huge expanse
of galloping strand, where its skirts are
swilled by the tide. Except that those
spires pre-date anything Disney ever did
by 1,000 years and have stood up to
centuries of storms, even though the
engineering skills required to perch them on their rock would severely
stress today's computer-assisted engineers. Besides, these days,
you'd never get the planning permission.

But you do need to pick your moment to visit. When did any
Disney or *Da Vinci* hero ever approach a mysterious, isolated
monastery on a sunny lunchtime, only to find there was no room in
the car park? Mont St Michel is France's biggest single tourist
attraction outside Paris, and occasionally in summer its narrow
lanes are virtually impassable.

Mont St Michel is a romantic vision, a dramatic tumble of tiles
that adhere like limpets to a rock, while high-speed tides gallop
hither and thither over surrounding quicksands. It needs to be
visited in a season when it rises mythically out of the mist, to a
soundtrack of howling winds and lashing rain, when for a moment

you might mistrust your eyes; is it real, or a trick of the windscreen wipers? You won't get that experience if the foreground is littered with tour buses. Make sure you choose a hotel within the island walls (see *Practicalities* below).

The experience begins back in Portsmouth, where Brittany Ferries' MV *Bretagne* is preparing to sail for St Malo. Overnight cross-Channel ferries get an odd cross-section of customers in the winter, and this one is no exception. On board, the hardened Francophiles are easy to spot, keeping their own company and ignoring the chips. The romancing couples are curling up in each other's laps. A crowd of forty-something designer-shirted males talking about 'tasty motors' are a group of golfing roofers who've prospered in the loft conversion era and are embarking on an invasion of Norman greens.

Next morning it's a short tootle from St Malo to the Mont. In the old days the island's pilgrims had to cross treacherous sands, and many were sucked under. Nowadays a causeway is causing sand to build up and the tide doesn't surround the island as it used to. There's been talk of cutting the causeway back to restore the integrity of the place and let the tide do its bit, providing access instead with a cable car. But for the moment you can still drive out to the front door.

Within the walls, one main lane winds up through a medieval village of beamed and gabled inns, restaurants and souvenir shops – some of them open all year – emerging eventually at the entrance of the abbey itself. From here there's a huge view of the draining bay covered in stripes of water, and you can watch for the incoming tide, described by Victor Hugo as moving with the speed of galloping horses.

At its lowest the tide retreats a massive 14km across the sands, to return at 4km/h – not quite galloping horses, but enough to terrify a party of Belgian tourists who had to be airlifted to safety one summer. Occasionally it covers the car parks, too, which recently embarrassed a British coach driver who was too busy with one of the hotel girls to notice the water rising.

Such shenanigans are hardly appropriate for what started out as a refuge of hermits and became one of France's most significant pilgrimage sites. At its peak, 500 years ago, there were 60 resident Benedictine monks (today there are just two), and daily waves of pilgrims made the treacherous sand crossing. The island's religious element has been swamped by commercial tourism, and only wintertime restores some of its original identity.

The huge fortified abbey – started in the 13th century and constantly enlarged – is impressive in any season, but more so with a wind whistling around and with only gargoyles for company. It's a massive feat of engineering that would look like a medieval multi-storey car park if you removed its walls; the huge granite church has been perched on a peak of rock, and beneath its floor is stacked a labyrinth of crypts, scriptoriums and refectories.

Most visitors spend an hour in the abbey, buy their souvenirs and leave, but you've come in winter, and you're here to stay. Two or three of the hotels down by the main gate will be pleased to offer you a room, and the lanes outside will be deserted as soon as night falls, with only the wind, rocking the street lanterns, for company. It's the sort of place where you'd expect to meet a hunchbacked Benedictine in a cassock, walking his Pekinese.

This weekend simply demands wild weather. The Mont is practically vertical with perhaps more roofage per acre than your average city centre, so a drop of the wet stuff has to make a Herculean effort to get down the back of your neck.

Snatch a dry moment, however, to venture out onto the causeway after dark. The island is at its visual best from here, lit up from skirt to spire like a Gothic rocket straining at its earthy foundations in a vain attempt to get to heaven. Billows of rain swirl around its rooftops and the occasional seabird is blown in from the dark for a moment of celebrity in the harsh pool of light, before being swallowed up by obscurity again. Such is life.

PRACTICALITIES

GETTING THERE

Brittany Ferries

❭ *0870 536 0360; www.brittany-ferries.com*

Daily overnight crossings from Portsmouth to St Malo even in winter. The return journey will be a daylight sailing, unless you want to come back via Caen. From £199 return.

TOURIST INFORMATION

❭ *+33 2 33 60 14 30; www.ot-montsaintmichel.com*

ACCOMMODATION

La Vieille Auberge $ $ $

❭ *+33 2 33 60 14 34; www.lavieilleauberge-montsaintmichel.com*

Inside the island walls.

Hotel du Mouton Blanc $ $ $

❭ *+33 2 33 60 14 08; www.lemoutonblanc.com*

Also inside the island walls.

THE TROPICS IN
A ZEPPELIN HANGAR

8

A BIZARRE ONE, THIS. A FORMER ZEPPELIN HANGAR
ON A DISUSED MILITARY AIRFIELD NEAR BERLIN HAS
BECOME HOME TO AN ALL-WEATHER TROPICAL RESORT.
MY TROPICAL ISLANDS IS LIKE NOTHING ELSE IN THE
WORLD. IT HAS A SEA, A LAGOON, A RAINFOREST,
ASIAN RESTAURANTS AND A HOT-AIR BALLOON, AND
YOU CAN OVERNIGHT IN TENTS ON THE SAND.

A RATHER FORBIDDING DISUSED MILITARY AIRFIELD IN
former East Germany is the last place you'd
expect to find a slice of the tropics. Especially a
resort where families of the under-dressed sit
back to watch a troupe of spangly bottomed,
feather-boa'ed Cuban dancers go through
an elaborate routine on islands in a
supposedly tropical sea.

NIEDERLAUSITZ

But there they are, those families,
lolling on sun loungers in their
swimwear, pina coladas at hand, toes in the sand and children in
the lagoon. To their left is a Balinese gateway and to their right a
hill crested with tropical rainforest. In front of them the 'sun'
(actually a projection on a giant screen) is just going down and the
ambient temperature is a luxuriant 28 degrees. Meanwhile, in the
distance over their left shoulders, you can just see new arrivals
pulling off their woolly hats and dusting the snow off their boots. It
is blowing a hooley outside.

Lagoons, rainforest and Balinese gateways are not exactly the norm
on disused airfields in Germany, and nor do you get many of them in
many other places in central Europe. But these are just some of the
features of an ersatz tropical resort which has been created a short
train journey southeast of Berlin, inside what is effectively a massive

greenhouse, complete with under-sand heating. And a whizzy weekend here certainly takes the edge off a long hard winter.

By now most of us are familiar with the new generation of public leisure pool, where swimming areas are landscaped with slides, waterfalls, seating areas and the odd plastic palm. So think of your local leisure pool, and then multiply it by a zillion, add sandy beaches, diving schools, campsites and a generous slice of the Eden Project, and you're beginning to get the idea of My Tropical Islands.

The resort is the audaciously ambitious creation of Malaysian businessman and millionaire Colin Au, who decided to 'bring the tropics to where they are needed most', ie: to central Europe in winter. Consequently it tends to attract people who might not be able to afford the long-haul trip for real, but there is also another great saving to be made here: by choosing not to take that long-haul flight, you are doing your bit towards saving the world.

From the outside, the chosen location doesn't bear much resemblance to anything tropical. The world's largest self-supporting hall, a giant palace of glass, rises amidst disused missile silos. It's a massive hangar originally built for a cargo-carrying zeppelin project called Cargolifter which went belly-up a few years ago, just before becoming operational.

Inside, the 'resort' is separated into distinct zones. Immediately obvious are the rainforest – partly created by consultants from Britain's Eden Project – and the two water areas. One is the Balinese lagoon, with waterfalls, rivers and jacuzzi pools; the other, the South Seas, is four-times Olympic size and has several islands plus a sandy beach and is surrounded by 720 deckchairs, backed by a bar and fine dining restaurant.

The heating for all this comes from under the floor and is very noticeable as you pad around barefoot. However it doesn't always penetrate, as you'll discover when you step from the warm floor onto cold sand; sand absorbs heat, refusing to pass the underfloor warmth on to the customer.

Elsewhere, the interior of the hangar is so large that a hot-air balloon takes (paying) guests on tethered 'flights'. Its launch pad is down at the leisure end away from the rainforest, where it is surrounded by sand-based volleyball courts, trampolines, paddle boats and bouncy castles. Not far away are more bar complexes and the various restaurants, all built in Thai, Malaysian and Indonesian architectural styles. Here you can have a brave attempt at a Peking duck or a Thai green curry, rendered absurdly mild for European palates. If you prefer to eat local there's plenty of beer and *wurst*.

The main sound stage, with jazz and rock bands at regular intervals, is amongst these oriental restaurants. But every evening there's a glamorous show staged out on the islands on the South Seas, once the sun has set on giant screens on the other side of the water.

Currently the evening show is a Cuban extravaganza, with 35 genuine Cuban dancers high-kicking, strutting and drumming their way around the South Seas islands, complete with feathery headdresses and bottoms like J-Lo. Along with fountains, dry ice and laser lighting, the show alone would normally have carried a hefty admission price, but it is free to all guests. The performers, however, do struggle with the dreadful acoustics of the airship hangar, which mangles most of the sound.

Overnighters rent tents down in the sandy area at the back of the oriental restaurants and next to the volleyball zone, which makes it hard to sleep when a group of lads is on court at three in the morning. But My Tropical Islands is honest about this. It points out that, as a 24-hour resort, it can't guarantee an undisturbed night. The lights stay on, the pools and bars stay open, and you can go for a swim if you want at 04.00, in the sure knowledge that there'll be a lifesaver on duty if all that lager and currywurst get the better of you. And where else can you do that in Europe?

PRACTICALITIES

GETTING THERE

Air Berlin

↘ *0871 500 0737; www.airberlin.com*

Return flights from Stansted to Berlin Tegel. Expect to pay around £90 return.

German Railways (Deutsche Bahn)

↘ *0870 243 5353; www.bahn.co.uk*

Catch a train from Berlin Hauptbahnhof to Brand (Niederlausitz) station, a journey of around 45 minutes. A shuttle bus to the hangar meets every train.

TOURIST INFORMATION

Germany Tourist Board

↘ *0207 317 0908; www.germany-tourism.co.uk*

Local tourism

www.wohlsein365.de/

My Tropical Islands ⑤

↘ *+49 35 477 605 050; www.my-tropical-islands.com*

Entry by the day or entry plus overnight accommodation in a tent.

9

PUSH-BIKE THROUGH PASTORAL MALLORCA

GET THOSE KNEES INTO THE BALEARIC BREEZE, CYCLING DOWN RURAL LANES IN MALLORCA'S LESSER-KNOWN INTERIOR DURING A SEASON WHEN THE ALMOND AND ORANGE BLOSSOM DISPLAY IS AT ITS BEST. BASE YOURSELF AT A FORMER MONKS' INN IN POLLENSA, NOW A QUIRKY, HANDSOME, EIGHT-BEDROOM HOTEL.

MALLORCA IS DIVIDED INTO MOUNTAIN — THE SIERRA Tramuntana runs right along the northwestern coast – and plain. The former hosts the hillside villages and citrus groves where royals and rock stars have their *fincas*, while the latter is fringed by the major tourist resorts where the hoi polloi spread themselves out to fry. Away from the coast, however, the plain can be surprisingly unspoiled, and it is largely ignored by the millions of tourists who flock to the island every year. Cyclists, however, know it well.

MALLORCA

At the beginning of spring – March onwards – Mallorca's rural lanes become a blaze of fast-moving lycra as European cycle clubs pass through on their training camps. They cross the plain in garish meteor showers, heads down over the handlebars and working hard, noticing little of the landscape in their rush to get to the other side.

En route they sweep past the occasional deviant; a cyclist who is happy to sit up and go slow, peering over dry stone walls into orange groves and almond orchards, winking at the sheep, smiling at the rabbits, startling a stalking cat and greeting an old gent picking wild asparagus on the verge. That cyclist, I suggest, is you.

Certainly the temperature – sunny but not hot – is perfect for pedalling, and personally I can't see the sense in going head down and full steam ahead when the island is looking its best. There's a lot to relish by the roadside, much of it a pleasant surprise. You're going to miss it if you've got sweat in your eyes.

The first real pleasure is in how carefully worked the land turns out to be. Despite the fact that the serious money lies in hotels, bars and property deals, the Mallorcan heartland is still quilted with almond orchards, vineyards, goat pasture and olive groves, and it is still all carefully looked after. You can't enter or exit a village without passing a man talking to his goats or a woman at the quarter-to-six position amongst her vegetables, both of them straight out of the supporting cast of *The Vicar of Dibley*.

The second pleasure lies in the undulations and urbanisations. The lanes of the plain dip and bob through a gentle sea, crested by villages that look white from a distance, but turn out on closer inspection to be built of a sort of pinky-yellow stone that is soft on the eyes. Notable amongst them is Sineu, surprisingly grand, perched on a hill, and happily impenetrable to cars. It feels pretty darn local, but the peace and quiet is partly down to second homes, and local shops stock *The Daily Telegraph*.

The third pleasure is in the hotels. Forget the characterless white blocks by the beaches, where everything is pre-packed. Ignore the tremendously upmarket country retreats in the hills, where film stars hang out with Arab princes. Between the two are lovingly created pocket-sized establishments which are personable, friendly and stylish. The sort of places you'd never notice existed, unless you're on a bike.

The one I recommend is in immaculate Pollensa, a perfect little town where every cobble seems to have been carefully polished, and every other shop is an artist's studio. Again, there are a lot of outsiders with houses here, and one of the restaurants (La Font del Gall) promotes 'contemporary cuisine with a Scottish twist', complete with haggis and neeps.

The Posada de Lluc, however, is totally homegrown and family run. A gem of a medieval townhouse that once accommodated monks, although they'd been long gone by the time of the development of the patio with the swimming pool surrounded by banana trees. Not to mention the sofas and the library of English books.

But don't be tempted to go to ground in the hotel; there's plenty of variety of landscape very accessible from Pollensa, down lanes marked as cycle routes by the tourist board. One day you can set off southwards towards Sa Pobla amongst orange groves and almond orchards; by lunchtime you're amongst fields of artichokes and potatoes in a flat land studded with old windmills around the village of Muro; by early afternoon you turn north into the Albufera, a secret reedy marshland filled with waterbirds you'd never expect to find on a hot Spanish island; and then finally you emerge into the touristy seaside by Alcudia, with its burger bars and duty-free shopping.

The next day you can head north through a gap in the Tramuntana, starting in suburban countryside on Pollensa's northern edge, where arty foreigners have their delectable *fincas*. By elevenses you'll be by the beach in the gorgeous cove at Cala Sant Vicenç, still very quiet at this time of year. And if you feel like more, you can retrace your route and head southwest along the flank of the Tramuntana, in a far starker land of olive groves and dry stone walls, passing some of the island's most upmarket properties as you go.

On the whole you won't go very fast or very far on your weekend, and most of the time you'll be overtaken by everyone else, but don't let that get you down. Those serious cyclists will all have gone to bed early, having supped on liquid energy. They won't be haggis-powered; they won't have dawdled over a bottle of red in one of the cafés on the Plaça Major, and they won't be climbing the 365 cypress-lined steps that lead up from the centre to the Calvari church. It's dark, of course, but from up here you can still follow the progress of a marching band, practising for some festival or other, thumping its way through town.

PRACTICALITIES

GETTING THERE

Several airlines have inexpensive flights to Mallorca, including **British Midland** (☏ *0870 607 0555; www.flybmi.com*). Expect to pay around £150 return.

Bus service 340 runs between Palma and Pollensa; schedules can be found on *http://tib.caib.es/index.en.htm*.

A **taxi** direct from the airport will be much quicker, but will cost upwards of €60.

TOURIST INFORMATION

The **Mallorca Tourist Board** has cycle routes on its website *www.illesbalears.es*.

TOUR OPERATOR

Several UK tour operators organise packaged cycling in this area. Try **Headwater Holidays** (☏ *01606 720099; www.headwater.com*).

CYCLE HIRE

In Port de Pollensa from **Rent March** (*carrer Joan XXIII, 89;* ☏ *+34 971 864 784*). Or else ask in the hotel, they are well used to dealing with cyclists.

ACCOMMODATION

Posada de Lluc $ $

☏ *+34 971 535 230 – or direct number from the UK;* ☏ *0871 218 0971; www.posadalluc.com*

A TASTE OF THE SAHARA

10

THE DATE-PALM OASES OF SOUTHERN TUNISIA
BORDER THE SAHARA DESERT. *STAR WARS* AND *THE
ENGLISH PATIENT* WERE FILMED HERE, AND TODAY'S
VISITORS CAN STAY IN THE CAVE HOTEL THAT
DOUBLED AS LUKE SKYWALKER'S HOME. WITH A
FLIGHT CONNECTION IN TUNIS, JOURNEY TIME FROM
LONDON IS UNDER SIX HOURS.

DEEP, DEEP IN THE GRAND ERG, THERE'S A STRANGE
encampment in the creamy Saharan mist, a
cluster of curious anthropomorphically shaped
eggbox habitations blasted by wind and sand.
From a distance it could almost be that
antique ruin out of Shelley's poem
Ozymandias, an empty, ageless symbol of
a civilisation long gone. Hard to imagine
that this is only a weekend break from
Britain.

SAHARA

On closer inspection, though, all is not as alien as it at first
seems. The curious eggbox habitations prove to be all plaster of
Paris on chicken wire. And civilisation is still lingering in the form of
a couple of hardcore groupies from Bristol, striking poses with light
sabres and quoting from the holy of holies (not the Koran, but the
original *Star Wars* script of 1977). For this is Mos Espa, the city
created by set designers for the first episode of the *Star Wars* trilogy,
The Phantom Menace. Not such a long time ago, and not in a galaxy
so far away.

Certainly the landscapes of southern Tunisia – desert, rock, salt
lake and searing sun – are alien environments to human habitation,
ideally suited to science fiction. But this is by no means the only
genre to find fertile ground in aridity; *The English Patient* was filmed

a couple of leaps further into the Erg (with the cave scenes in a nearby phosphate mine). Then there was Spielberg's *Raiders of the Lost Ark*, Zeffirelli's *Jesus of Nazareth*, and Python's *Life of Brian*, along with a raft of less well-known productions. It is not just the unnatural landscapes that make the region such a happy hunting ground for film makers; everywhere you go there are faces and costumes ready-made for the camera.

For *Star Wars*, sets like the one at Mos Espa were modelled on the local *ghorfa* or fortified grain store architecture and costumes were fashioned after the local flowing robe, the *burnous*. Even the names were influential, with Jedi named after the nearby island of Jerba, and the arid planet of Tatooine after the desert city of Tatouine.

Over the years the crews and stars for all these films have stayed in the local oases, Douz and Tozeur. Hotels were built to cater for them and their groupies, and the tour groups who followed the groupies. So now, from having been a sleepy, mud-brick oasis town, Tozeur is a substantial resort in the desert with daily flights from Tunis and onward connections to London, which adds up to a pretty weird weekend.

The influx of money means that much of Tozeur's delicately patterned adobe brickwork has been intricately restored. However these days most of the 40,000 date palms in the *palmeraie* are ignored, because tourism is a far more rewarding crop. Nevertheless the *palmeraie* is a peaceful place of filtered sunlight, and it twitters and rustles, while old men lurch down foot-hardened paths patched with squashed dates seeking fresh grass for their donkeys. The whole place smells of wild flowers, woodsmoke and horse dung, and although the hotels have robbed the trees of much of their water, this is still the place where the locals come to enjoy the cool of the evening over fermented palm juice drunk out of earthenware cups. A bit naughty, if you are a good Muslim.

Douz, on the other side of the giant salt lake of Chott el-Jerid, is less of a resort than Tozeur, although a lot of visitors come through here *en route* to spending a couple of hours on camelback heading out into the dunes. It too has its own film sets, one a mud-brick fortress built for an Italian-made Western, and the other a surreal recreation of Paris half submerged in sand for a Jean-Paul Belmondo film called *Peut-être*. Remember *Ozymandias*? 'Nothing beside remains. Round the decay/of that colossal wreck, boundless and bare/The lone and level sands stretch far away.'

Southeast of Douz the Ksour begins, where the landscape rears up like wrinkled elephant hide, caked with ochre earth and hairy with eucalyptus. If you get this far, the old fortified grain store of Ksar Haddada in Tatouine was another of the locations used in the making of *The Phantom Menace*. Until recently it was one of the world's most peculiar hotels, a honeycomb of crazy living, the creation of dwarves who thought they were bees, but decay – and scavengers – has set in.

You can, however, still stay at another extraordinary hotel with a longer association with *Star Wars*, not far away.

From ground level, the village of Matmata looks unexceptional, but an aerial view reveals a series of crater courtyards of troglodyte pit houses, many of them still inhabited, the underground rooms pleasantly cool throughout the fierce summer heat.

Amongst them is the Sidi Driss, a hotel with 26 rooms cut into monks' cells off its four crater-courtyards. It featured in the 1977 film as Luke Skywalker's home, and in the cave bar there's a good chance of meeting *Star Wars* groupies. Either way, this must be one of the strangest places in the world for dinner (couscous, naturally), bed & breakfast, and it is not for the faint-hearted when it comes to the shared toilet arrangements.

Outside the Sidi Driss's couscous, you eat what you can get in these parts. When I was last here, I travelled with a local guide who bought camel meat in the local market and took it into a nearby shanty restaurant for cooking. It tasted excellent, but when we'd finished, he looked at me. 'You realise,' he said, 'that camel is an aphrodisiac, and we should make love before we sleep'. There was nobody there but we two – and the camels.

PRACTICALITIES

GETTING THERE

Tunisair

☎ 020 7734 7644; *www.tunisair.com*

Biggest choice of flights, plus a monopoly on the internal flights from Tunis to Tozeur (usually one or two hours' connection time in Tunis Airport); expect to pay £340 return.

British Airways

☎ 0870 850 9850; *www.ba.com*

Returns to Tunis from £175, and then Tunis/Tozeur with Tunisair costs £69 return.

TOURIST INFORMATION

☎ 020 7224 5561; *www.cometotunisia.co.uk*

CAR HIRE

Avis

☎ 0870 606 0100; *www.avis.co.uk*

Drivers must be over 21.

Europcar

☎ 0870 607 5000; *www.europcar.co.uk*

Drivers must be over 21.

Travel agencies in Tozeur offer the option of 4x4 vehicles plus driver/guide.

ACCOMMODATION

Hotel Sidi Driss S

☎ +216 75 24 00 05

Reservations are not necessary.

Wigmore Holidays

☎ 020 7836 4999; *www.aspectsoftunisia.co.uk*

Offer several hotels in Tozeur.

11
TENERIFE'S HIGHER LOWER ISLE

THE CANARY ISLAND OF TENERIFE HAS LARGELY
SURRENDERED ITSELF TO TOURISTS AND DEVELOPERS,
BUT THERE IS ONE CORNER WHICH RETAINS TRACES
OF ORIGINAL ISLAND CULTURE, WITH A TOWN THAT
HAS COME BACK FROM THE DEAD.

ANYONE WHO ARRIVES IN TENERIFE THESE DAYS
expecting some kind of rural paradise with a
fascinating indigenous culture will realise their
error as soon as they glimpse the temple of
Ikea by the airport. The island's sunnier south
coast, where most of the package tourism
is located, is scrubby, arid and looks like
a giant cat litter tray. Meanwhile the
north coast is largely residential and
hugely overdeveloped.

Most of the island is lassoed by a single motorway which is
treated like a racetrack by young *tinerfeños*. But there is a point on
the circuit where those ribbons of tarmac merge into one and the
new villa projects fall away. This is the northwestern corner, known
misleadingly as Isla Baja, or Lower Island.

'Lower' is hardly the right description for this craggy shoulder of
land. Some of Tenerife's most remote villages are lodged in its
steepling ravines, along twisting roads not for the nervous (or
carsick) passenger. Most notable is the remote hamlet of Masca,
with stunning views out to Gomera. Of course lots of visitors come
here – every other house in Masca is either a restaurant or a gift
shop – but you'll soon shake them off if you take the ravine path
down to the sea, taking care not to tread on the lizards.

But the place I'd particularly draw your attention to for a weekend in
Isla Baja is Garachico, 25km west of Puerto de la Cruz, and the last

town of any size on the northern coast. In the 17th century this was the island's premier port, exporting Malmsey wine to England and sugarcane and cochineal throughout Europe. A prosperous place of grand merchants' houses with the churches, convents and monasteries that those merchants endowed to keep their consciences clean.

According to legend, the Church–merchant relationship started the whole problem, after the town was cursed by the personal chaplain to a powerful nobleman. The chaplain's influence over the household had grown so tyrannical that the nobleman was forced to dismiss him. The holy man responded in a very un-Christian way: 'Garachico, rich town, waster of wealth, let an evil rock fall on you!' And guess what.

Whether you believe in monkish curses or not, Garachico's position on a little instep of land beneath Tenerife's volcano Mount Teide was always going to be vulnerable, and in 1645 heavy rains caused a landslide which killed 100 people and buried 40 ships. Undeterred, the merchants excavated and rebuilt – only to have their work ruined 61 years later when Teide erupted. This time the lava flow was slow enough to allow people to escape, but it slid, hissing and bubbling, into the harbour, filling it up. Ending Garachico's *raison d'être* just like that.

Since then the town's dusky grandeur has barely changed. The fine buildings are all still there, surrounded by terraced vineyards and banana plantations, and for many decades difficult land access deterred the burgeoning overdevelopment that has afflicted much of the island. The result is a peaceful little gem of cobbled streets and Canarian architecture, with a central square surrounded by laurel trees, a Franciscan convent, an 18th-century church, and the residence of the Counts of Gomera. By day groups of old men play cards under the laurels; by night, it'll be all lit up just for you and the convent cat.

No other seaside town in Tenerife is so unblemished, although the modern world has arrived somewhat incongruously in the shape of a giant swimming pool and football stadium, right by the sea. The original damage is only visible when you venture down to what used to be the port. Here fiercely jagged waves of lava are threaded by new paved paths, and in a couple of locations there are deep pools, used by swimmers. A little 16th-century fortress stands to one side, some distance from the water it was built to control, and there's a little patch of black sand.

Garachico's renaissance in tourism terms has come about thanks to a couple of lovely boutique hotels which occupy two of the grandest houses. On the main square stands the Quinta Roja, a quirky conversion of the former home of the Lord Bailiff of Tenerife, with a galleried inner courtyard and a whirlpool bath on the roof. Some of the rooms still have the old peephole shutters, and you can sit behind them on wooden window seats and eavesdrop on salty conversations below. The Quinta Roja is owned and run by a lively group of thirty-something siblings, one or other of whom is usually around.

The San Roque nearby, is more snobby. Also a conversion of a patio'ed merchant's house, it is chic and artistic, and anyone with a keen eye will spot designs by Le Corbusier and Mies van der Rohe amongst the DVD players and flat-screen TVs. Clientele commute the short distance from the breakfast room to sunbeds by the pool or on the roof terrace, picking up that day's newspaper on the way. Here, the whirlpool baths come with every room.

This is the quality end of Tenerife, and visitors have a sense of having made a discovery on an over-discovered island, in a part that the mass market has yet to reach. Accordingly they are happy to stay local, making short expeditions to unspoilt Canarian landscapes and eating in the likes of Garachico's tiny Lagar de Julio Restaurant, where a chef who used to be a fisherman offers cod and rabbit. Most of the local restaurants will also serve one of the island's truly original dishes, *papas arrugadas* (wrinkly potatoes). They're boiled in their skins, crusted gently with salt and served with a spicy tomato sauce. Simple, but quite delicious.

PRACTICALITIES

GETTING THERE

British Airways (☏ *0870 850 9850; www.ba.com*) and **Monarch Airlines** (☏ *0870 013 3123, 0870 040 6300; www.flymonarch.com*) both have frequent direct flights from as little as £85 return.

TOURIST INFORMATION

www.webtenerife.com

CAR HIRE

All the usual suspects, plus local agency **Cicar** (*www.cicar.com*). Starting price around £30 per day.

ACCOMMODATION

Hotel Quinta Roja $ $
☏ *+34 922 133 377; www.quintaroja.com*
Hotel San Roque $ $ $ $
☏ *+34 922 133 435; www.hotelsanroque.com*

THE GAMBIA, WHERE DIRT POOR MEETS PACKAGE TOUR

12

ACCESSIBLE, TROPICAL AFRICA FOR A LONG WEEKEND, STAYING IN AN ELEGANT FLOATING LODGE OFF A CREEK ON THE RIVER GAMBIA, SURROUNDED BY MANGROVES. YOU'LL NEED TO TAKE ANTIMALARIALS, BUT WITH THE GAMBIA ON THE SAME TIME ZONE AS THE UK, THERE'LL BE NO JET LAG WHATSOEVER ON YOUR RETURN.

IT BARELY SOUNDS POSSIBLE, AND YET WITHIN SIX HOURS of taking off from Gatwick on a grey and greasy winter morning you could be up a creek in west Africa.

THE GAMBIA

You'll be sitting on the balcony of your own floating lodge. Around you, nature will be in full riot mode, with the whole food chain right from the fiddler crabs to the fire finches operating at a level of intensity that only persists in undeveloped parts of the world. The sunset will be flickering off the water, the creek exploding with fish and the sky veined with African egrets, returning from a day in the rice fields.

A pair of giggling Mandinka women will come scudding past on the rising tide, their hand-carved pirogues piled high with freshwater oysters. As they pass they will greet someone behind you, someone whose feet have just started to pad down the wooden walkway to your lodge. It's the chef, come to enquire whether you'd prefer the ladyfish or chicken yassa for dinner. No chips or schnitzel here.

This is the tiny west African country of The Gambia, famous for a history of slavery, for having more birds per acre than any other country – and for a bizarre interface between dirt-poor Africa and package-tour Europeans seeking winter sun.

Till recently, most of The Gambia's tourism development has been concentrated in an enclave of sizeable and unappealing hotels on the beach. It makes an uncomfortable mix, Africa and fly-and-flop package tourism, so big is the contrast between rich and poor. It has also earned itself a reputation for sex tourism – in this case single white women (aka Marie Claires) who come to meet local men, who apparently give them something they can't get at home!

This type of package tourism is not exactly Bradt territory, but there is a growing community of smaller, more characterful lodges, which definitely are.

The best example is Mandina, the floating eco-lodges surrounded by laughing doves and malachite kingfishers, barely 20 miles from the airport, but light years away from the world of aviation.

Anyone who has been on safari in Africa will recognise the concept, but Mandina is the first luxury safari-type lodge to appear in west Africa, and it is very much a labour of love. Most of the love, and a great deal of the labour, is down to two Englishmen, Lawrence Williams and James English, who arrived here 12 years ago and bought a scrap of land with the intention of setting up a backpackers' rest.

So intent were Williams and English on getting everything right that they spent seven years living in a tent on the land they'd bought, planning, planting, and integrating with the local community. In the end they acquired 1,000 acres of the monkey-rich forest, complete with resident palm-wine tapper and *marabout* or holy man. Thereafter they substantially upgraded their accommodation plans, and the result is inspirational: a sinuous pool, a jetty, a bar and restaurant made from rhun palm and malinda wood, with floating and stilted lodges each with a guide and its own dugout canoe. And all for a maximum of just 12 guests.

You don't come here for the party atmosphere, that's for sure – although the baboons can make quite a racket. It's a place to chill, to sit by the creek, greet the singing fishermen and let the tide wash away the stress of urban life. There's something bizarrely satisfying about being in exactly the same time zone as the UK; 09.00 in shivering London is shorts and fruit salad time on the Bolong Mandina, prior to pushing off in your canoe.

Guides will suggest excursions: on water there's fishing for barracuda and captain fish, and dawn and sunset paddling on the creek; on land there's birdwatching trails and a walk in the woods to where the palm-wine tapper lives, for a cup of milky liquid which tastes like semi-fermented ginger beer.

Mandina is set in the Makasutu Forest, with nature trails, wildlife trips and a clearing where craftsmen work and sell their products. Tour groups come in here daily and local villagers prepare lunch and sing for them; packaged cultural experiences like this are not always to be recommended, but this one is well done, and if you're here only for the weekend, it provides an accessible way of getting to grips with Gambian village life.

One of the most pleasing things about Mandina is that it is not an expatriate transplant. Many safari camps feel as if they've been teleported into Africa via Fulham, with white faces in key positions. But Williams and English, busy with new projects, largely leave it to their local team to run the lodge. The result is occasionally eccentric – an hour's wait for a salad – but it works.

Mandina does have a couple of in-built disadvantages: it is not cheap, and is often full. If either of those proves a problem but you're still keen to try The Gambia for the weekend, then book yourself in at the Safari Garden in Fajara, run by another very energised British couple, Geri and Maurice Phillips. Set in a small compound within walking distance of the beach, their motel-style place has its own pool and restaurant, with cakes (beetroot and chocolate a speciality) made by Maurice. While you're there, ask them about their own eco-project, the Sandale Eco-Retreat, on the coast down towards the border with Senegal.

PRACTICALITIES

GETTING THERE

Direct flights from London Gatwick are operated by XL Airways but sold by tour operator Gambia Experience's flight arm, **Gambia Flights** (☏ *0845 330 2063; www.gambiaflights.co.uk*). Expect to pay around £450 return.

TOURIST INFORMATION

☏ *020 7376 0093; www.visitthegambia.gm*

ACCOMMODATION

Mandina $ $ $ $
The Mandina lodges are bookable via the website www.makasutu.com, or via tour operator Gambia Experience (☏ *0845 330 2060; www.gambia.co.uk*), who will arrange flights and transfers.
Safari Garden Hotel $
Fajara
☏ *+220 449 5887; www.safarigarden.com*

OTHER PRACTICALITIES

Don't attempt to hire a car. Taxis are cheap.
You may only be going for a weekend, but you still need to arrange antimalarial prophylaxis, usually either Lariam, Malarone or doxycycline. Consult your GP.

SPRING

Spring is in the air. The British countryside is beginning to look good, but you wouldn't want to linger too long in any one spot. Herefordshire's Golden Valley has a mix of sheltered and wild walking either in bucolic countryside or up on Offa's Dyke; the air is champagne-fresh along Northumberland's Coast & Castles Cycling Trail; and if you need a bit of inner warmth before tackling these outdoor activities, then join the Pudding Club for a weekend in the Cotswolds, and get on the outside of jam roly-poly and friends. (*HOME FRONT* 13–15)

Just across the Channel there's a health-enhancing experience waiting for you around Brittany's seaweed riviera, Finistère, famous for wild weather and plump onions. Less health inducing is a road-based weekend to the Nurburgring in Germany, where you can pilot your own car around a race track that professional racing drivers decided was too dangerous back in the 1970s. Alternatively head out for Transylvania, where the motor vehicle has yet to overhaul the horse and cart as a method of transport of choice, and stay with a Transylvanian Count. And there's another hospitable Count closer to hand, near Hungary's inland sea, Lake Balaton, where the eastern bloc used to take its holidays.

Spring is a great time for cycling, so I've two recommendations here: the first is a route in Baden-Württemburg that links Baroque towns and a river that emerges from a hole in the ground; the second is a route in the Loire Valley, but one where you actually stay in a château and avoid all the tourists. And finally, my most southerly suggestion for this season is a railway route across the sunny side of the Alps which stitches together two of Slovenia's most attractive lakes, Bohinj and Bled. (*MEDIUM DISTANT* 16–22)

For a foretaste of summer sun, I'm recommending a whizzy weekend to Egypt's Red Sea, which is not as costly as you might think. There's more sun to the far west on the Canary Isles's most remote outpost, El Hierro, which is something of a surprise cultural experience. And there's even more sun on Norway's Lofotens, where the midnight sun kicks off at the beginning of May. (*Further Flung* 23–25)

PRICE GRADING FOR ACCOMMODATION

$ – up to £40 for a double room; $$ – £40–70 double;
$$$ – £70–110 double; $$$$ – £110 + double.

DESTINATIONS

HOME FRONT

MEDIUM DISTANT

FURTHER FLUNG

13

HEREFORDSHIRE'S BUCOLIC BUFFER ZONE

SPRING IN GOLDEN VALLEY, HEREFORDSHIRE. THIS
IS THE BUFFER ZONE BETWEEN ENGLAND AND WALES,
ONCE PRONE TO CROSS-BORDER RAIDS AND A
SANCTUARY FOR MEN ON THE RUN, INCLUDING THE
DISGRACED NOBLEMAN WHO INSPIRED
SHAKESPEARE'S FALSTAFF. SLEEP WHERE HE SLEPT,
AND WALK THE BORDER RAIDERS' PATHS AT OFFA'S
DYKE, ALONG THE EDGE OF THE BRECON BEACONS.

IN THE COMPELLING, BITTERSWEET FILM *SHADOWLANDS*,
the author C S Lewis (played by Anthony
Hopkins) has a picture of Herefordshire's
Golden Valley hanging on his study wall. It
starts the film as his image of heaven, but by
the end of his fated love affair with American poet
Joy Gresham (Debra Winger) – she dies of cancer
– it has become a symbol for elusive joy. It's a
potent image to hang around the neck of any
destination.

The valley in question runs diagonally southeast
from Hay-on-Wye to the A465
Hereford–Abergavenny road, where it is
sandwiched between the frowning flank of the Black Mountains and
the wide-screen sumptuousness of the Wye Valley. At first sight it is
British countryside without any of the bells and whistles; no great,
glorious views, eminent ruins or tumbling cataracts, just an
undulating mesh of lanes cast over a tissue of farmland where cattle
gently graze. Its name derives, not from any glamorous physical
characteristics, but from the name of the river – the Dore – which
runs through it (*d'or* = of gold, in French).

It is not a major tourism destination. And yet, once you've been there a couple of days, you begin to appreciate the understated power of the place. It stands alone, buffered by impenetrable lanes from the rest of the world, with its own sense of self-sufficiency. A long history of border raids and medieval fortification against the marauding Welsh have conferred a certain independence of mind on those who live here. If you climb up onto the darkly forbidding flank to where Offa's Dyke marks the Welsh border, and look east to see what the raiders saw, the valley may even look golden.

Within the wider area is some of the finest British walking and a couple of real classics of church architecture. Dore Abbey is the only former Cistercian abbey church still in use, and although it was badly shorn of most of its structure during the dissolution of the monasteries, there are still reminders of late 13th-century grandeur, and the footprint of its former glory lies on the ground all around.

By contrast, the small flagstoned church at Clodock, which is mostly 12th century, has been left completely unmolested, and remains wonderfully atmospheric inside, with tiny Norman windows in the northern wall, ancient box pews and a 17th-century orchestral gallery.

The Golden Valley's oldest stonework is Arthur's Seat, a Neolithic burial chamber near Dorstone, with a wonderful view. Other notable stone structures are the 12th-century motte and bailey castle at Longtown, originally built by one Walter de Lacy to provide protection for his livestock, wives and children against border-crossing ruffians. Having built the castle, he then also made a tidy sum from the 800 villagers, who could only shelter here if they paid a fee.

And talking of fee-paying shelter, try to stay in Olchon Court, a wonderful 14th-century farmhouse which once provided sanctuary for the discredited Sir John Oldcastle, Shakespeare's model for Falstaff. This must rate as one of the finest bed and breakfasts in the country, although there's a rumour that it is up for sale.

The Valley is laced with footpaths. An easy pastoral route climbs across fields from Dorstone via Arthur's Seat to Merbach Hill, which overlooks the Wye Valley.

More adventurous, and when weather conditions allow, is the Olchon Valley's Black Hill, whose ridge footpath joins up with the Offa's Dyke long-distance footpath after three miles. Black Hill's first peak has views in all directions and a jumble of rocks that provides relief from every prevailing wind. But once you reach Offa's Dyke, you'll be stepping into a bleak peaty world inhabited by partridge, grouse and merlin. Turn south and you'll eventually come upon an intersection with a pile of stones, where a path dives back into the pastoral valley below where you started.

The advantage of Golden Valley is that it isn't on the coast, isn't in commuting distance of anywhere (apart from Hereford and Hay-on-Wye) and doesn't grab headlines. The result is that not every handsome property has been bought by urban folk seeking rest and recreation, and there's still a strong local community. For the visitor, the net result is encounters with the sort of inspirational British eccentricity which only flourishes, like the most delicate of wild flowers, in an unsullied, unselfconscious landscape such as this.

Examples are Hedley Wilding, now very elderly, but still running his front garden petrol station in Vowchurch. Then there's the twin-brother hill farmers of the Olchon Valley, who could so easily be character models for Bruce Chatwin's novel *On the Black Hill*.

And finally don't miss the Gwatkin family, who run Abbey Dore Farm Shop on the B4347 north of Abbey Dore and who could be straight out of *The Darling Buds of May*, although without any visible Catherine Zeta Joneses. In the shop you can get the likes of boiled fruit cake and rose petal wine, as well as the Gwatkin's own cider and excellent beef and lamb. Outside, amongst the barrels in the yard, geese, dogs and aged relatives watch the shoppers come and go.

PRACTICALITIES

GETTING THERE

Golden Valley lies between the A465 and the A438 west of Hereford, which also hosts the nearest railway station (*www.nationalrail.co.uk*).

TOURIST INFORMATION

Hereford

✆ *01432 268430; www.visitherefordshire.co.uk*

ACCOMMODATION

Olchon Court S S

One of several Golden Valley B&Bs, searchable on *www.golden-valley.co.uk*.

The Old Post Office S-S S

Llanigon

✆ *01497 820008; www.oldpost-office.co.uk*

A colourful, creative, vegetarian B&B in a building which started life in the 17th century as the village pub.

PLACES OF INTEREST

Dore Abbey

www.doreabbey.co.uk

14

CUSTARD-FEST IN THE COTSWOLDS

A WEEKEND AT THE PUDDING CLUB, BASED IN THE
THREE WAYS HOUSE HOTEL IN THE COTSWOLD
VILLAGE OF MICKLETON. WALK THE HEART OF
ENGLAND WAY BY DAY, AND REFUEL BY NIGHT WITH
AS MANY HELPINGS OF SPOTTED DICK AS YOU CAN
ACCOMMODATE. THE PUDDING RECORD IS 19
PORTIONS.

THERE'S A DISCREET FRATERNITY AMONGST THE
ROLLING hills and yellowstone houses of the
Cotswolds. It's a club which, despite being out
of step with the modern age, has proved
surprisingly popular. Its members gather regularly,
seeking inner warmth in the frostier times of year
from a commodity which, although not quite on the
banned substance list, is rarely mentioned in public.

During these meetings members gather round a
high table on which are laid bubbling cauldrons, and
although the concoctions therein are not exactly sinful,
they do fall into the category of 'naughty-but-nice'.
Happily, the Great British Pudding is far from extinct.

The Pudding Club was founded in 1985 to prevent the demise of
traditional favourites like jam roly-poly at a time when restaurants
were going alarmingly nouvelle cuisine. Over the years it has
increasingly found favour amongst people who want more than just
drizzle for dessert. Based in the handsome Three Ways House
Hotel in the Cotswold village of Mickleton, it holds meetings up to
twice a month, and the only criteria for membership is a deeply felt
passion for pud.

Mickleton is a pretty little place in the land of Chippings, Sods and
Burys. The surrounding hills are laced with walking routes, and local

shops groan with local meat, fruit and vegetables. It isn't, however, honeypot Cotswolds, and its attractions are fairly specialist. A couple of miles south, for example, adjacent to the Heart of England Way, is Mickleton railway tunnel, where the great engineer Brunel was involved in what is usually described as the last pitched battle between private armies on British soil: Brunel's gang of 3,000 navvies took on the army of disgruntled contractor Mudge-Marchant, who refused to proceed with digging the tunnel until he'd been paid.

These days, the only real bunfight in Mickleton is when the pud-lovers come to town. The Three Ways House Hotel itself looks much like any other, although a handful of its rooms have been especially decorated to celebrate particular favourites. For example the Sticky Toffee room has been decorated in Moroccan style in honour of the dates and demerara sugar in the recipe, and a resident guest who wakes in the middle of the night, slightly disoriented, will be even more so when he reads of the need to mix Camp coffee with butterscotch sauce, all written on a camel's backside.

Despite the name, you don't have to be a member to attend a Pudding Club evening, and nor do you have to be unduly large. Aficionados – usually 70-odd for this banquet with custard – gather beforehand in the hotel lounge for a glass of fizz and to listen to a pud briefing. There's a kind of camaraderie amongst them, and although most have never met before, conversation flows. Veterans of previous meetings compare tactics and mutter darkly about ratios of sponge to fruit; and none of the hardcore would have eaten anything during the day.

In the dining room everyone sits at long tables, and the master of ceremonies lays out the rules of engagement. Start with the less rich, he advises; and go easy on the sauces or you won't last the distance. Everyone on a table has to clear their plates before anyone can return for the next, and there's a token first course that must be dispensed with first.

Then they're off, one table at time, tackling the mountains of syrup sponge, rice pudding and rhubarb and ginger crumble, with lashings of custard or chocolate sauce. In between mouthfuls a large, cheerful gentleman informs all around him that his absolute favourite recipe comprises a tin of rice pudding, a bar of Galaxy and a glass of Cointreau, all mixed together. When that hits the stomach, he declares, it makes the brain disengage.

Apart from a rush for the skin on the rice pudding (real connoisseur stuff) everyone settles into their stride. By pudding number five or six (lemon sponge followed by coffee and walnut cake) some of the field begins to falter. One of the fillies puffs out her cheeks, pushes away her jam roly-poly, and announces that no further sweetmeat will pass her lips, but that she could murder a pickled herring.

Eventually a couple of the veterans are the only ones still going, and the large, cheerful gentleman is telling everyone that it was the second course of the squidgy chocolate and nut which did for him. But even the veterans fail to get past ten puds, a poor effort compared to the record holder, a 15-year-old boy who'd managed 19.

Needless to say, he hadn't had a comfortable night, and I dare say that, at breakfast the following day, he had difficulty looking a slice of black pudding in the eye.

PRACTICALITIES

GETTING THERE

Mickleton is six miles south of Stratford-upon-Avon on the B4362. The closest rail connection (*www.nationalrail.co.uk*) is Evesham.

TOURIST INFORMATION

❭ *01452 426 280; www.cotswolds.com, www.mickleton.com*

ACCOMMODATION

Three Ways House Hotel $ $ $ $
Mickleton
❭ *01386 438429*
Pudding Club evenings
www.puddingclub.com
Pudding Club £24/head (aperitif, main course and seven puddings). Membership not necessary. Two-night pudding breaks, including pudding evening and evening meal in the hotel's main restaurant from £165 per room/night.

NORTHUMBERLAND'S COAST AND CASTLES

15

THE COAST & CASTLES CYCLING TRAIL IS A PRIME
STRETCH OF THE NATIONAL CYCLE NETWORK ALONG
BRITAIN'S EAST COAST, STARTING IN EDINBURGH AND
ENDING IN NEWCASTLE. *EN ROUTE*, IT PASSES EMPTY
BEACHES, SALMON SMOKERS AND RUINED CASTLES.
AND WHEN YOU RUN OUT OF STEAM, THERE'S ALWAYS
A COAST-HUGGING TRAIN TO REWIND THE FILM.

BERWICK-UPON-TWEED IS ONE OF THOSE PLACES THAT
can't quite decide whether it wants to be
economically successful or to settle for just
being attractive. Straddling the England–Scotland
border at the mouth of the viaduct-spanned river
Tweed, it still has a functioning port, and the
pleasing aesthetics of its downtown architecture are
somewhat smothered by neon and traffic. But it is a
good place to begin a journey on two wheels, and
end it on multiples of four.

NORTHUMBERLAND

On a good day the Tweed Estuary is all swans on a
summer morn, with the occasional plashy salmon
showing its delight at encountering fresh water at
last. There's likely to be a rust-bucket of a grain coaster doing a slow
pirouette out by the harbour wall, and a pair of old wooden cobles
will be lying on the grass by the Berwick Salmon Fishery sheds,
suggesting that fishermen up here still do it the hard way. It could
be a scene from any time in the last 30 years, were it not for the
black-liveried GNER high-speed train thundering over the viaduct.
Your route here and back again.

South of Berwick, the Coast & Castles Cycling Trail hugs the shore
along a narrow ribbon of a sheep track with sandy bays, seals and
surf on one side, the susurration of daisy-rich grassland underneath

one's tyres, and the occasional scything London to Edinburgh express beyond. The National Cycle Network's avowed intention is to avoid busy roads at all costs, and this section certainly does that.

At Cocklawburn the cliffs descend to dunes, the foreshore broadens and you can cycle out across immaculate hard sand to sit by the sea. A nature reserve sign says 'Welcome to Philadelphia' – the Philadelphia with the three 18th-century lime kilns, not the young upstart in America.

The castle bit of the Coast & Castles Cycling Trail starts at Bamburgh. In Anglo-Saxon days this was the capital of Northumbria, the castle rearing high on a lump of basalt above village, dunes and sea, and dominating all horizons. Remodelled by a family of northern industrialists who, in their time, made practically everything you can make with metal, its offbeat museum holds an assortment of wrecked flying machines, dredged up in the nets of trawlers working off the coast.

Glance offshore and you might think they'd hauled in a few wrecked ships, too. The Farne Islands look like capsized supertankers, and many a vessel has come to grief on these semi-submerged shelves of rock. When a paddle steamer called the *Forfarshire* was wrecked here back in 1838, the alarm was raised at 04.45 by a lighthouse-keeper's daughter called Grace Darling, whose saccharine name belied her determination and oarsmanship. She and her father set out in a rowing boat to rescue the survivors, an act of bravery which inspired dozens of romantic Victorian paintings. Some are displayed in the village's Grace Darling Museum.

The four miles that separate Bamburgh and Seahouses could be 400, so little do the two places have in common. Bamburgh – immaculate, with cottage tea rooms, country inns and a cricket pitch; Seahouses – unappealing, with amusement arcades and chippies, although this is also the place to get a boat out to the bird-rich Farne Islands.

Back on the cycle route, Dunstanburgh is the most ruggedly romantically ruined of all the castles, and can only be reached on foot. From a distance it looks impressively fortified, but centuries of exposure in such a spectacular coastal site have taken their toll.

A mile-and-a-half further south is Craster, a tiny harbour with two crab-like claws of concrete which vainly try to retain the ebbing tide. As an anchorage it plainly has seen better days, but there are still a couple of larch-planked cobles which set out from here for the salmon fishing, for this is the only open-water driftnet fishery left around Britain's coast.

Craster may seem a peaceful scene, but this has been the setting in recent years for an age-old battle between the classes. On one side were the professional sea fishermen, who had the licences to net salmon, and on the other the posh rod-and-line river fishermen, for whom catching salmon is a cherished hobby, who lobbied hard to have the sea fishery closed. In the end there's been a compromise, with the rod-and-line community offering large amounts of money to buy the driftnet licences, and most of the driftnetters have felt unable to refuse.

Nevertheless some local salmon still end up in Robson & Sons' smokery, just up behind the harbour. Robsons started up 100 years ago, producing kippers from the fish landed by the long-gone fleets of Craster herring boats. Today the raw material comes from Iceland (the country, not the frozen-foods retailer), but Robsons have kept going, and are currently the chief suppliers of kippers to quality supermarkets.

They also supply the kippers that are served for breakfast on the GNER, and it is time you too thought of catching the train, so head for Alnmouth, where all the fast trains stop.

It'll take GNER 20 minutes or so to rewind your labours of the last two days back to Berwick. It's odd, watching your hard-won landmarks gobbled up like that, but you will be the only passenger who could name all the coastal villages flying by, and have the kippers to prove it.

PRACTICALITIES

GETTING THERE

Berwick is on the A1 and the London–Edinburgh main line (*www.nationalrail.co.uk*).

TOURIST INFORMATION

Berwick

☎ *01289 330733; www.northumberland.gov.uk*

CYCLE HIRE

Tweed Cycles
Berwick

☎ *01289 331476*

Around £25 for two days. Cycle route details can be found on *www.coast-and-castles.co.uk* and *www.sustrans.org.uk*.

Cyclists intending to retrace their steps on GNER trains need to reserve cycle spaces in advance when they buy their tickets.

ACCOMMODATION

Pack Horse Inn S S
Ellingham

☎ *01665 589292; www.thepackhorseinn.org.uk*

16

BRITTANY'S
SEAWEED RIVIERA

WEED TOURISM IN FINISTÈRE. THALASSOTHERAPY AU
NATUREL IN THE HOME OF THE SEAWEED INDUSTRY,
ROSCOFF, ON THE COAST OF BRITTANY. THIS IS ALSO
THE SPIRITUAL HOME OF CRÊPES, ONIONS, JOHNNIES
AND THE CHEAPEST SPA THERAPY IN WESTERN EUROPE.

THE END OF THE WORLD IS FULL OF WEED. SEAWEED.
It comes in all varieties, shapes and sizes, and
some of it is surprisingly handy.

This particular end of the world – *finis-terre* –
is the French one, Finistère, the one that used
to feature on the shipping forecasts. The
one that wrestles with the Atlantic at the
western end of Brittany, hurling rocks at
passing ships. Round here the maritime
authorities position an emergency tug
offshore at the first sign of high wind, just in case. Remember those
posters of huge waves engulfing lighthouses you had when a
teenager? That's Finistère.

This last gasp of France is a sort of Cornwall with *pastis*. And
unlike the majority of French landscapes, which come in broad
sweeps of the painter's brush, it is an intimate place of sturdy
granite villages and slate-roofed cottages. On the land it's ideal
territory for growing vegetables, while under the sea the huge tides
are brilliant for *Laminara digitata* – a seaweed whose extracted
alginates are used in the manufacture of cosmetics, toothpaste,
paper, medicines, yoghurt and ice cream. To mention a few.

Seaweed tourism may sound an unlikely idea, but the various
bodies involved in the largest seaweed-producing area in Europe
have created one of the most unusual trails in European tourism. A
sort of Seaweed Riviera.

The weed industry started with local farmers wading fully clothed into the sea with a rake to collect organic fertiliser for their vegetables. *Digitata* grows on underwater rocks where there's a particularly strong tidal flow, making this one of the most dangerous forms of harvesting in the farming world.

It was made safer in the 1970s thanks to something called the *Scoubidou*, on display in the Maison de L'Algue ('seaweed house') in the tiny fishing and weed-collecting village of Lanildut. Despite its exotic name, the *Scoubi* looks like a giant version of a dentist's toothpick, worked with a corkscrew action. Its purpose is to pluck three-year-old *digitata* off underwater rocks, twirling it round like spaghetti, and its name derives from a Sacha Distel song about 'apples, pears and *scoubidous*' which in those days were plastic bangles kids wore round their wrists. This simple device is at the heart of an industry that supplies around 11% of the world's weed, and a skilled *Scoubidou*-ber leaves the seabed stones unturned, to allow new weed spores to grow.

A visitor following the weed industry from village to village will travel through some of Finistère's finest scenery. From the Baie des Anges at Aber-Wrac'h, a giant bowl of water where there's always something with sails scudding around, to the promontory opposite Ile de la Vierge, host to the highest lighthouse in Europe. But in the end you're bound to end up in Roscoff, the charismatic home of Brittany Ferries.

The company started here as a tiny operation run by farmers who wanted to bring their weed-enhanced vegetables to the UK, and these 'Johnnies' (as in 'Johnny Foreigner') would ride around the West Country on bicycles with onions draped over the handlebars.

The Johnnies have gone (their passing recorded in the unlikely sounding 'Maison des Johnnies', by the station), but the town is still a delightfully rural little place, where the main concern is still the size of one's onions. On the seafront there's a busy fishing harbour, a little seamen's chapel and a small ferry to Ile de Batz offshore. The town hall is decorated with strings of onions, the church bell tower looks like a load of old pots and pans balanced in a pile, and the lanes are full of crêperies and fish restaurants.

Roscoff is also a weed-seeker's nirvana – shops even sell seaweed beer – with a very advanced weedy visitor centre as well as one of the world's earliest thalassotherapy spas.

The visitor centre is Thalado, Centre de Découverte des Algues (literally 'centre for the discovery of weeds'), and it does everything imaginable with weed, from collection walks to cookery demonstrations. Static exhibitions reveal that there are thought to be 40,000 different species of weed, but we've only studied 1,000 of them in any detail, so we don't yet know how beneficial they all may be. We do know, however, that weed produces between 50% and 70% of the planet's oxygen, which is handy.

Just across the road is the Thalassothérapie Institute Rockroum, one of Europe's oldest seawater spas. It originally opened in 1899, and still has the lingering ambience of a sanatorium, but is also very good value in today's spa world. For £70 you can have a 'discovery' half day of four or five treatments, including a saltwater hose-down, where you're told to face the wall by a white-coated woman with a powerjet, as with the riot police. More gentle are the seaweed bath – sharing a vat of hot water with a giant teabag – and seaweed wrap, for which you are painted all over with weed paste and then wrapped in clingfilm to brew.

After all that you stagger out smelling a bit like something washed up by the tide. Do check, however, that you haven't acquired any extra fauna or flora along the way. Barnacles will grow in any secluded crevice given half a chance.

PRACTICALITIES

GETTING THERE

Brittany Ferries
☎ *0870 366 5333; www.brittany-ferries.co.uk*
Sail daily from Plymouth to Roscoff. Expect to pay around £235 for a return plus car and berth.
Flybe
☎ *0871 700 0535; www.flybe.com*
Has flights to Brest for around £100 return.

TOURIST INFORMATION

www.discover-brittany.info

ACCOMMODATION

Hotel La Baie des Anges $ $
Port de l'Aber Wrac'h
☎ *+33 2 98 04 90 04; www.baie-des-anges.com*
A cross between a boutique hotel and a seaside B&B.

PLACES OF INTEREST

Thalado (Centre de Découverte des Algues)
5 rue Victor Hugo, Roscoff; ☎ *+33 2 98 69 77 05; www.thalado.fr*
Thalassotherapie Institute Rockroum
☎ *+33 8 25 00 20 99; www.thalasso.com/roscoff*
Discovery sessions with four treatments and use of spa pool for around £70.

17

PETROLHEAD PARADISE AT THE NÜRBURGRING

PUT YOUR PEDAL TO THE METAL ON GERMANY'S ORIGINAL GRAND PRIX TRACK, BUT BE CAREFUL, THIS IS NOT A VIDEO GAME. NICKNAMED 'GREEN HELL', THE NÜRBURGRING WAS REMOVED FROM THE FORMULA ONE LIST AFTER NIKI LAUDA'S HORRENDOUS ACCIDENT BACK IN 1976.

FOR A COUPLE OF WEEKS EVERY YEAR 'ELEPHANTS' roam around the volcanic hills of the Eifel region. You can glimpse the beasts through the trees, drawn up in silent circles in the gloaming, their leather-clad riders gathered around camp fires swapping stories and roasting *bratwurst* on the embers.

It could almost be a scene from *The Jungle Book* (apart from the bit about the *bratwurst*) but the Eifel is not India, and these 'elephants' are not four-legged with tusks, but two-wheeled with chrome. 'Elephant' is the collective name given to large motorcycles of a mature age, particularly BMWs, and for a couple of weekends a year the Eifel hosts thousands of elephant owners who come to camp in the hills and compare upholsteries. A stay which culminates in a boy-racer ritual where bikes, sports cars, family saloons – and even busloads of tourists – demonstrate that they still have what it takes.

This fir-cloaked region of rolling hills close to the Belgian border is a paradise for petrolheads, thanks to one of Europe's most famous motor-racing circuits, the Nürburgring. The Ring is the circuit which Jackie Stewart christened 'Green Hell', and you can drive around it in your own set of wheels, if you dare.

In the beginning, back in the early years of the 20th century, there was only the one racing circuit at the Nürburgring. The 14-mile Nordschleife drapes itself in sinuous loops over the Eifel's forested peaks, and in its day it was a wonderful track in an admirable woodland setting, but over the years the cars simply became too quick for its 73 right-angle bends. The drivers began to voice their concerns in the 1960s, but it wasn't until Niki Lauda was badly injured in an accident in 1976 that they finally clubbed together and refused to compete there again.

Since then the Nürburgring has opened a second, state-of-the-art Grand Prix track which hosts Formula One every June, but the Nordschleife is still there. Much of the time it is used for specialised testing, but on selected days (usually at the weekend) it is opened to the general public, which puts a new spin, literally, on a Sunday-afternoon drive. Vehicles of all shapes and sizes sally forth, their drivers keen to unleash their inner Audi and see what they, and their car, can do.

A circuit like this is unrelenting, a ribbon of tarmac sliding around in a pool of green and presided over by the 12th-century Nürburg Castle, peering snootily down over the treetops. The adrenalin surge of driving here renders the experience quite distinct from belting along a normal country road, but don't get carried away. Never mind that all traffic is heading in the same direction; there's always an overtaking meteor shower of BMWs and Porsches to contend with, and while you might be driving well within yourself, the others may not.

You will be informed, before you set out, that it is your responsibility to pay for any damage you might do to crash barriers. But frankly, if you ever find yourself hauling out the credit card, you should be pleased you're not dead.

There is an alternative to putting your own wheels through hell: take one of the most unusual taxi rides in Christendom, with the sort of *taxista* that a chap's dreams are made of. Sabine Schmitz, a cool blonde dressed in soft leather, is one of three drivers of the Ringtaxi, the latest generation BMW. She follows exactly the same route as all the elephants and the family saloons, but this time at speeds of up to 160mph, with only a touch on the brakes for the 73 right-angle bends.

In under ten minutes she'll reduce her passengers to putty without resorting to terms of endearment or putting her hand on anyone's knee. She'll be chatting away blithely as if this sort of thing happens several times a day – which of course it does.

In the end you don't have to put either yourself or your own set of wheels through Green Hell if you don't want to. Over by the Grand Prix track is the Nürburgring's Erlebniswelt, an adventure world which simulates and celebrates motor racing. It starts in building one with a museum of classic and famous racing vehicles before moving on to a whole hall of video games based on motor racing in building two, with scientific examinations of the properties of tyres in the basement. Building three is dedicated to BMW, hosting exhibitions, films and driving simulators, and building four has an indoor go-kart track plus a fascinating solar-powered vehicle circuit where you can take control of the light source (ie: the power) and the steering.

If all of that is not enough and you still want to kick ass, then release yourself onto the German *autobahn* system in the world outside, which has no official speed limit. Germany has none of our angst about automobiles. It likes them shiny, big and fast – and, like the elephants, it gives them freedom to roam.

PRACTICALITIES

GETTING THERE

The Nürburgring is 390 miles southeast of Calais, and almost due south of Bonn. Local towns are Adenau and Kelberg.

TOURIST INFORMATION

Germany Tourist Board
☎ 020 7317 0908; *www.germany-tourism.co.uk*
Local tourism
www.wohlsein365.de

ACCOMMODATION

Ringhaus Altes Forsthaus $ $
Nürburg
☎ +49 26 919 353 90; *www.ringhaus.com*
Only 200 yards from the Nürburgring entrance and run by motor-racing fans.

NÜRBURGRING INFORMATION

Official website (Tourist Info Zentrale am Nürburgring) (☎ +49 26 913 026 20; *www.nuerburgring.de*). Information on daily opening times. Nordschleife circuits in your own car from £13 (£43 for four).
Useful UK website for Ring enthusiasts (*http://nurburgring.org.uk*).
Ringtaxi
☎ +49 26 919 320 20; *http://ring-taxi.bmw-motorsport.com*
£120 per circuit (up to three passengers).
Elephant reunion (Altes Elefantentreffen)
www.alteselefantentreffen.de

STORYBOOK TRANSYLVANIA

18

STAY WITH A TRANSYLVANIAN COUNT IN THIS
MYTHICAL LAND OF FORESTED HILLS IN PASTORAL
ROMANIA. COUNT TIBOR KALNOKY'S GUESTS STAY IN
A STORYBOOK VILLAGE IN A HORSE-AND-CART SOCIETY
WITH BEARS IN THE WOODS AND WOLVES IN THE
HILLS AND WHERE THE COWS BRING THEMSELVES
HOME AT MILKING TIME.

TRANSYLVANIA (LITERALLY 'THE LAND BEYOND THE
forest') is the most unspoiled landscape in the
whole of Europe. Communities here still rely on a
barter economy, bake their own bread, distil
their own plum brandy, heat their houses with
firewood and live in ethnic villages of
Hungarian, Romanian and even German
origin, with storks on chimney stacks and
hand-cranked waterpumps on street
corners. It's a fragile environment just
waking up to tourism.

Count Kalnoky's estate is not far from the historic city of Brasov,
in the village of Miklósvár. This is a sleepy little Hungarian-speaking
settlement of subsistence farmers and woodsmen, where there has
never been any recorded crime. The Count's manor house
dominates the village centre, but is under restoration and echoingly
empty other than on feast days and special celebrations.

The Count himself lives some kilometres away but his guest
accommodation is a little group of buildings 100m from the
manor, where the main reception house has a drawing room,
dining room, kitchen, and downstairs cellar used for dinner.
Elsewhere in the village is another clutch of oak-beamed
guesthouses gathered around a little courtyard, with oil lamps

and wood-fired heating, antique furniture and hand-embroidered textiles, as well as the latest in low-voltage lighting and fully equipped modern bathrooms.

Guest meals are prepared and served by the ladies of the village back in the reception building. They are based on local ingredients – pork stews, dumplings, fresh bread, cheese – and eaten either outside, under a vine terrace, at lunchtime, or down in the cellar around a big oak table.

Count Kalnoky presides over some of these meals. He is an urbane, sophisticated 40-year-old aristocrat with flawless English (as well as German, French, Hungarian and Romanian) and equally flawless manners, and not in the least bit scary. Although he is too modest to talk about it, his family pedigree dates back to the 12th century, and his great uncle Gustav was Prime Minister of the Austro-Hungarian Empire. He returned to Romania 12 years ago, after the downfall of communism, and since then he has been recovering and restoring previously confiscated family property. The paying guests create a revenue stream for himself and for the village, producing an economy which will encourage younger villages not to abandon traditional ways of life. He hopes.

One of the features of that traditional life is the daily cow parade, when a long string of straw-coloured cattle comes ambling down the main street punctually every evening at 20.00. Cows hereabouts are completely self-guided, taking themselves up to the grazing lands in the morning, and bringing themselves home again in the evening, peeling off when they reach their front doors to nose their way into family courtyards. All their owners need to do is to make sure the courtyard gates are open to let them in.

This daily cow parade is part of the village's proverbial social life, along with not counting your chickens until they hatch, and making hay while the sun shines. Every evening villagers sit outside their front gates, gossiping until the cows come home.

If you've got time to venture further afield, the Count has a handful of guides who lead bear-tracking and bird-spotting trips, plus horse-and-cart rides up to a picnic barbecue in the hills. The route is up through pastures to the fringes of a forest of beech and hornbeam, watched by wheeling birds of prey. There, on a hillside thick with campion, ragged robin, speedwell, purple coltsfoot and willowherb, they'll make a wood fire on which to grill steaks, which are then washed down with brandy.

Otherwise there are cultural trips to fortified churches, castles and medieval cities. Viscri, formerly known as Weisskirch, a village that was once completely Saxon and German-speaking, is relatively nearby. The guides can organise lunch at the house of one of the 26 remaining Saxon villagers before taking you up the hill to the medieval Saxon church, where the men still sit upstairs and the women downstairs. You'll likely also meet Saxon grandmother Sara Totz who still tolls the church bell at noon to tell the farmers that it is time to eat, because there are no wristwatches here. Your guides might also point out the house that Prince Charles recently bought in Viscri, although he'd rather the whole world didn't come knocking on his door.

And then of course there is Sighisoara, a Saxon and Hungarian town with cobbled streets and pastel houses piled up the sides of a hill to where a formidable citadel stands, its clock tower rising above the dusky red roof tiles. This is the birthplace of Vlad Tepes or Vlad the Impaler, the model for Dracula, and the place to find blood-sucking souvenirs. Bran Castle, where Dracula is supposed to have lived, is a day trip away on the other side of Brasov.

Count Kalnoky himself tends to downplay the Dracula angle. When quizzed on the subject he points out, gently, that Dracula is the product of an English writer's imagination, and that the people of Transylvania had never even heard of him prior to 1990, when Bram Stoker's work was first translated into Romanian.

So no need to pack the garlic.

PRACTICALITIES

GETTING THERE

Wizz Air (☏ *+48 22 351 9499; www.wizzair.com*) has returns from Luton to Bucharest for upwards of £100, but both **British Airways** (*www.ba.com*) and **Tarom** (*www.tarom.ro*) have more frequency for not much more cost.

Count Kalnoky can send a car to pick you up from the airport for £45 per person one way (three–four hours); otherwise take a train (*www.infofer.ro*) from Bucharest to Brasov and his driver will meet you there.

TOURIST INFORMATION

☏ *020 7224 3692; www.visitromania.com*

ACCOMMODATION

Count Kalnoky's Guesthouses $ $ $
☏ *+40 742 202586; www.transylvaniancastle.com*
Price includes meals and activities.

If you'd prefer, **Transylvania Uncovered** (☏ *0845 300 0247; www.beyondtheforest.co.uk*) works closely with the Count and can arrange all flights, transfers and accommodation.

19

BALATON, CENTRAL EUROPE'S SEASIDE

FOR DECADES LAKE BALATON HAS BEEN A MAJOR
CENTRE OF RECREATION FOR CENTRAL EUROPEANS,
ISOLATED BEHIND THE IRON CURTAIN. AND THERE'S
STILL GOOD STUFF HERE IF YOU CAN FIND IT —
WATERSPORTS, VINEYARDS, CASTLES — ALTHOUGH YOU
SHOULD AVOID THE FISH SOUP.

IN EARLY 2006 RYANAIR OPENED A NEW ROUTE TO
Lake Balaton, and its try-anything-once pilgrims
stepped out onto the tarmac of an airport that
was until recently only used by Russian war
planes. They probably thought they were
pioneering something new, but to be
honest anyone from central Europe could
have told them that Balaton is old hat,
and that most central Europeans, now
that they have the freedom, would far
rather take themselves off to Mallorca or Barcelona. If they had the
cash.

But Balaton has its interest, provided you approach it with some
awareness of its history. Moreover it has started to offer interesting
places to stay, if you know where to look.

The 77km-long lake is the largest in central Europe, and in the
days before European integration it was a magnet for Czechs,
Slovaks, Croats and Hungarians who couldn't go further afield. In
the 1960s and 1970s it acquired new significance as a rendezvous
for German families separated by the Wall, becoming the neutral
ground on which divided families could meet up and relax. That
emotional significance means that many older Germans continue to
come here for their holidays, and several have bought holiday
homes by the lake's edge.

The lake itself, although large, is never more than 2–3m deep. It warms up quickly in the sun, which makes it popular for watersports, although powered boats are not allowed. Its southern shore is flat and pretty busy, particularly with families and teenagers looking for nightlife in Balaton's equivalent of Ibiza, the resort of Siófok.

Its northeastern end is comparatively built up, too, being closer to Budapest, and this is where you'll find a mega Tesco, symbolic of the wonders of European integration. But its western end has vineyards on hills, unspoiled villages, a natural spa and a very pleasing university town. Fortunately, this is where Ryanair puts down.

The pleasing university town is Keszthely, the destination of shuttle buses from Balaton Airport. A leafy, pedestrian main street is lined with cafés, and it is here you need to beware of the fish soup: it's made with bottom-feeders who've gone a bottom too far. Somewhere along the main street you'll also find a David Beckham in marzipan (in the Marzipan Museum) and a Houses of Parliament in snails (that's Budapest's Houses of Parliament, and many millions of snails).

A more significant cultural attraction stands at the end of the street. Festetics Castle was the home of the Festetics family, and is unique in Hungary in that it remains intact inside as well as outside. All other aristocratic properties were ransacked during the communist era, but this one was preserved thanks to quick-thinking locals, who bricked up its entrance and attached a sign reading 'beware infectious diseases'. Inside there's parquet floors, ancestor portraits, gold-framed mirrors and chandeliers, and a library as large as a church.

Keszthely's hotels are down by the lakeside. The Hullam looks grand and traditional, but has dark, unreconstructed rooms. The Helikon next door is an unprepossessing 1970s' block, but with refurbished interior and gym, pool, spa and watersports facilities. At around £30 for a double, they are inexpensive for what they are.

There's more upmarket accommodation in nearby Hévíz which is built around a volcanic lake (actually more of an oversized pond). Changing rooms rise on stilts out of its slightly radioactive sulphurous water, which is pleasantly warm all year round. The pond might turn into a lake were it not for the fact that its spring also feeds the various hotels in the surroundings. These cater overwhelmingly to elderly German-speaking guests on spa cures, which are considerably cheaper here than at home.

But the best of Balaton lies beyond the urbanisations, in the rural hinterland, where it becomes a sort of poor man's Tuscany. Down to the south, one of the few aristocrats to return to Hungary – Count József Hunyády – has a pastoral guesthouse (Lehner Manor) from where he runs riding holidays. Those equestrian guests start and finish with the Count, dining with him and the French-speaking Countess, but in between they spend a couple of nights in the Somogy Forest at a hunting lodge called Háromházi Fogadó, hidden away down a sandy track and so rural that it is a wonder it gets any business at all. The Háromházi (nearest village Libickozma) has an indoor pool, sauna and restaurant and is open to anyone, not just hunters or horsemen. You're unlikely to get a better deal anywhere in Europe than the £9 a night (£30 full board) offered here. Provided you can find it, that is.

On the north side of the lake the most scenic region is called the Káli Basin, where rolling hills are interspersed with meadows and orchards. Here too are small village pensions of character, particularly those close to a volcanic hill called Badacsony, patched with vineyards, one of which, apparently, belonging to Gérard Depardieu. Here a narrow lane winds upwards towards a hilltop forest, passing roadside *dégustation* stalls and boutique wineries-cum-restaurants.

It is hard to resist a little refreshment or two as you walk up. By the time you reach the top, and the wonderful lake views from the terrace of Maison Kisfaludy (whose menu includes specialities like 'angler fish with crab stew') you will be in need of a good long sit down.

PRACTICALITIES

GETTING THERE

Ryanair
☏ *0871 246 0000; www.ryanair.com*
Flies to Balaton three times a week, for around £85 return.

TOURIST INFORMATION

☏ *020 7823 1055; www.balaton-tourism.hu*

CAR HIRE

Fox Autorent
☏ *+36 83 355 500; www.fox-autorent.com*
Has a desk at Balaton Airport; cars from £33/day.

ACCOMMODATION

Háromházi fogadó S
Near Libickozma
☏ *+36 85 714 002; www.haromhazifogado.hu*
Count Hunyady's B&B S S
Lehner Major, near Keleviz
☏ *+36 30 226 9553; www.hunyady.hu*
Hotel Helikon S S
Keszthely
☏ *+36 83 889 600; www.danubiushotels.com/helikon*

20

FROM THE ACH TO THE BLAU

THE GERMANS ARE PRETTY GOOD AT CROSS-COUNTRY
CYCLE ROUTES, AND THIS ONE IS PARTICULARLY
SCENIC, RUNNING AS IT DOES THROUGH WOODED
RIVER VALLEYS TO THE NORTH OF THE DANUBE. PAST
PRETTY TOWNS, PASTORAL LANDSCAPES, BAROQUE
CHURCHES AND A MIRACULOUS CISTERN WITH
MONASTERY ATTACHED.

ALL GERMANS WILL BE FAMILIAR WITH THE STARTING
point of this itinerary, thanks to a much-loved
tongue-twister 'In Ulm und um Ulm und um Ulm
herum', which basically means 'in and around
the city of Ulm'; *heruming* Ulm is pretty much
what I'm suggesting you do on this
weekend.

The city is an hour's train journey from
either Stuttgart or Munich (both have
cheap flights from the UK), and it sits on
the banks of the Danube where Bavaria borders Baden
Württemburg. Ulm is not Germany's prettiest city, which is our fault
for bombing it to smithereens in World War II; there was a giant
fortress and barracks here, and some parts of the walls are still
visible, discreetly absorbed into parks. According to the intriguingly
translated city brochure, this makes the city 'an Eldorado of modern
architecture'; the same translator describes Ulm-child Albert
Einstein as being 'at the very top of the list of go-getting Ulmites'.
Einstein a go-getting Ulmite? Now you know.

Anyway, much of Ulm has been carefully rebuilt and
pedestrianised, particularly the Fishermen's Quarter down by the
river, where visitors sit out on terraces and eat grilled trout. It's an
exceedingly pleasant place to hang out. If you've got time to spare

before or after your bike ride climb to the top of the cathedral spire, the tallest in the world at 161m, and quite a physical ordeal.

There's a bicycle-rental shop right by Ulm's main railway station. Once you've sorted your bike, head for the train, and don't be intimidated; all the local services heading to your destination, Riedlingen (usually one every hour) will take bicycles, for free. Look for the bike symbol next to the relevant carriage door.

Emerging in Riedlingen, you'll find a cobbled *altstadt* full of gabled and shuttered houses in a tight fist of alleys on the flank of a hill by the Danube, here still little more than an oversized stream. The half-gabled houses around its market square seem to bend a bit at the knee, a nod here, a curtsey there, and most days there are stallholders with local fruit, cheese, meat and vegetables.

The cycle-path distance from here back to Ulm is just under 70km, do-able in a day if you worked hard. But I suggest you take it slowly; there are plenty of gasthofs and pensions *en route*, and they're well accustomed to accommodating cyclists.

From Riedlingen, the route runs beside the river and is well signposted, but make sure you're heading downstream. After 30-something km it'll bring you into Ehingen, another handsome place with a *schloss* (castle) and a big market square. A good place to stay, and if the weather is good, head for the open-air beer garden in the park below the castle walls.

From Ehingen you need to find the Blautal cycle route, which breaks off the road that leads past the railway station. Now you're heading for Blaubeuren, and you'll be out amongst asparagus fields, where the earth is piled high in long rows and covered in plastic sheeting. The cycleway weaves through farm villages and wobbles from side to side across the narrowing valley, crossing and re-crossing the river Ach.

Blaubeuren is yet another handsome town, with carefully preserved 15th-century architecture threaded by the Ach, running in canals. But the big attraction is the Blautopf, at the far end of town. This is where the river Blau emerges effortlessly from a hole in the ground, so deep you can't see the bottom. The resulting Blautopf is a shimmering, azure lagoon surrounded by woodland, so calm that you'd never believe that it is filling (and flowing) at as much as 32,000 litres per second. This is the outlet for a whole underground river system, and at weekends you can sometimes see divers disappearing down into the Blautopf on explorative expeditions. They are still making discoveries of new cave systems down there.

As for the water colour, most days it is forget-me-not blue, but that can change; after rain, the blue turns lighter and cloudier, and after a lot of rain it can even turn green or yellow, as the power of the water releases yellow lime particles from below ground.

The Blautopf is, frankly, quite miraculous, so the presence of a Benedictine monastery next to it is no surprise; the late-Gothic (15th-century) double-winged high altar is unique in the world.

From Blaubeuren it's an easy pastoral ride back to Ulm along the banks of the Blau, which by now has absorbed the Ach with no signs of indigestion. The last couple of kilometres are rather unpleasantly urban; ignore the signs to Neu-Ulm, on the Bavarian side of the river, and you'll eventually be back in the bike-rich, car-free downtown, having successfully *herumed* Ulm.

PRACTICALITIES

GETTING THERE

Germanwings (☎ *0870 252 1250; www.germanwings.com*), **easyJet** (☎ *0905 821 0905; www.easyjet.com*), **Air Berlin** (☎ *0871 500 0737; www.airberlin.com*), and **British Airways** (☎ *0870 850 9850; www.ba.com*) all offer inexpensive flights to Stuttgart or Munich. Expect to pay around £120 return.
There are frequent trains to Ulm, see *www.bahn.de*.

TOURIST INFORMATION

German Tourist Board
☎ *020 7317 0908; www.germany-tourism.co.uk*
In Ulm
☎ *+49 73 116 1283 0; www.tourismus.ulm.de*

CYCLE HIRE

Rad Station
☎ *+49 17 515 002 31*
An unmistakeable building between the railway station and adjacent bus station. Hire will cost under £5 a day.

ACCOMMODATION

Crooked House Hotel S S S
Schiefes Haus
☎ *+49 73 196 79 30; www.hotelschiefeshausulm.de*
A charismatic place to stay in Ulm, if it's within your budget. It's in the Fishermen's Quarter, and is in the *Guinness Book of Records* for crookedness.
Gasthof zur Rose S
Ehingen
☎ *+49 73 917 556 26*
Central, clean and inexpensive.
Blank's Brauereigasthof Rössle S
☎ *+49 73 736 43; www.brauerei-blank.de*
Closer to Riedlingen, the handsome village of Zwiefaltendorf has a guesthouse in a brewery.

21

THE LOIRE BEYOND THE HANDLEBARS

CYCLING DOWN THE LOIRE VALLEY CAN BE DISAPPOINTING IF YOU DO THE OBVIOUS AND SIMPLY FOLLOW THE RIVER. THE LATTER IS, FRANKLY, DULL. BETTER TO FIND THE NEWLY CREATED CHÂTEAUX À VÉLO NETWORK, AND BASE YOURSELF IN STYLE AT A PROPER CHÂTEAU-HOTEL.

AS A 'VALLEY' THE LOIRE IS A BIT OF A FAILURE. THE word suggests something intimate and pastoral with sloping sides, but in this part of western France the land is pretty much flat, albeit with a thumping great river sliding through it. It doesn't have the grandeur of the Lot or the Dordogne and its interest lies primarily in the 800-odd châteaux along its length, 100 of which are open to the public. From a car, struggling with traffic jams, there won't be much to look at.

From a bicycle it's better. On two wheels, you'll dip into the occasional hamlet where farmers' wives will be on their knees amongst the vegetables. The air will smell of woodsmoke, there'll be kingfishers on the water, lapwings in the fields of corn, and a caterpillar on your shirt. None of which you'd notice in a traffic jam.

There'll be some of this pastoral detail on the Loire's dedicated cycle track, Loire à Vélo, a 150km stretch of an ambitious 800km European Rivers project (Nantes to Budapest) with a budget of a staggering £36 million – the sort of money which would otherwise buy a new six-lane motorway. But then the French are bonkers about cycling.

Loire à Vélo is, however, a linear route, which means it takes you from one place to the next along the riverbank, involving new accommodation and the movement of luggage every day. It is

possible to resolve these logistical problems with Accueil Vélo (bicycle welcome) accommodation, but it's all a bit much for a weekend. For that, you'd be better off tackling the more intimate Châteaux à Vélo network, and stay in one place – a place that will also provide you with a bicycle. Preferably a château.

Châteaux à Vélo has 11 different circuits on a mix of dedicated cycle tracks and very quiet country lanes in the Sologne region to the southeast of Blois. Each route is around 15–30km long, each carefully signposted, and each different from the other. Each requires basic map-reading skills to complete, but then that creates the additional excitement of a treasure hunt, where mindlessly following a massive river does not. The creators have given these routes romantic names like *Ombres et lumières* (shadows and light) or *La balade à rémonter le temps* (cycling back in time), but most are pretty rural, with some sort of château or *manoir* somewhere along the route.

The landscapes here are more undulating than on the banks of the Loire. Here you're in a patchwork landscape of little vineyards and cornfields, interspersed with oak woodlands and dotted with villages with chickens and churches. Apart from big names Blois, Chambord and Cheverny, all on Châteaux à Vélo routes, this is the territory of the private château, lots of them (18 in the village of Cellettes alone). Here you'll explore the Loire backwaters on a more human scale, through a land of aristocrats who are still trying to keep the roof repaired. And here, unlike in the Loire Valley proper where châteaux tourism is such big business, you can cycle right up to the front door.

One of the finest examples of owner-occupations is the Renaissance palace at Villesavin, with its 14th-century spit system in the kitchen and bizarre collections of chamber pots and 'wedding glasses', figurines in glass cases, in the outhouses. Villesavin, run these days by Mme Baudet du Poitou, was built by Jean le Breton, Minister of Finance to King François I, using the same workmen (and possibly the same budget) as were employed on François's own seriously large second home at nearby Chambord.

Villesavin is one of very few châteaux to still have a towering dovecote. In their day these were hugely symbolic buildings, with the number of nesting holes in the walls corresponding to the amount of land owned – and tax paid – by the Lord of the Manor. Accordingly, during the French Revolution, most of these dovecotes were destroyed by the mob as symbols of hated ownership. Even today, the keeping of birds in old dovecotes is forbidden. Mind you, you can still find a dish in local restaurants which translates as 'pigeon in rat purée', but don't be alarmed, 'rat' is a variety of potato.

There are two other pleasures I'd point you towards in the Châteaux à Vélo network. One is the local viticulture in the Cheverny region, known for the excellence of its white wine. Small owner-operated vineyards like Domaine de la Champinière by Cour-Cheverny on Châteaux à Vélo Route Four have bottle sales and tastings which may well necessitate a snooze under a nearby hayrick before you pedal on.

The other is the characterful places to stay, and I have one particular one in mind: the Château de Breuil, just outside Cheverny and also on Route Four. A lot of the Château-hotels in the Loire are stuffy and unwelcoming to cyclists, but Breuil is not, despite the (slightly faded) grandeur. In fact, this is the place to borrow your bike, from the hotel's own collection in the shed.

Despite definitively welcoming cyclists, Château de Breuil is not your normal cyclist's accommodation, and you will need to bring a set of clothes in which you feel comfortable when you sit down in the drawing room. But there's no greater pleasure, after a hard day in the saddle viewing other people's properties, to return to your own temporary residence which also has its own woodland, swimming pool and turreted bedrooms with four-poster beds.

PRACTICALITIES

GETTING THERE

London to Tours with **Eurostar/TGV** (☏ *0870 518 6186; www.eurostar.com*) costs from £79 return and takes six hours. Regular local trains shuttle between Tours and Blois.

TOURIST INFORMATION

French Tourist Office
☏ *09068 244123; www.franceguide.com, www.loirevalleytourism.com*

CYCLE ROUTES

Full details of the Châteaux à Vélo cycle routes are on the website *www.chateauxavelo.com*.

ACCOMMODATION

Château du Breuil $ $ $
Route de Fougères, Cheverny
☏ *+33 2 54 44 20 20; www.chateau-du-breuil.fr*
Cycles available at the château.

BLED AND BOHINJ, TOO BEAUTIFUL FOR MURDER

22

TAKE A RURAL RAILWAY ACROSS THE TOP OF
SLOVENIA, THE MOST PEACEFUL OF THE FORMER
YUGOSLAV NATIONS. STAY OVER AT BOHINJ, THE
MOUNTAIN-SURROUNDED LAKE ONCE DESCRIBED BY A
HOLIDAYING AGATHA CHRISTIE AS 'TOO BEAUTIFUL'
TO BE INCLUDED IN ONE OF HER BOOKS.

THE LITTLE-KNOWN BOHINJSKA MOUNTAIN RAILWAY
meanders through the sunnier southern side of
the Alps, connecting Jesenice by the
Slovenian/Austrian border with Gorizia and
Trieste in Italy. Originally built by Austro-
Hungarian royalty who wanted to holiday
by much-loved vineyards and lakes, it is
something of a feat of engineering, with
no fewer than 43 tunnels in its length,
including one that's 6,237m long.

LAKES BLED
AND BOHINJ

But you don't have to be a trainspotter to enjoy the trackside view
of steep valleys, hayricks, brightly painted beehives and onion-
domed churches. This is rural Slovenia, a neat republic of
mountains and vegetable patches wedged between Italy, Austria and
Croatia. And here the train halts briefly at villages full of scratching
chickens and grannies with zinc pails.

Of all the countries that were once part of Yugoslavia, Slovenia has
fared the best. As a previously little-known nation it has remained
relatively unspoiled and relatively inexpensive. Moreover it is part of
the Slovenian character not to oversell oneself, which means that
when you get there you realise that the place is just as good – if not
better – than you expected. A rarity in today's well-travelled world.

The part of Slovenia stitched together by the Bohinjska railway is a
case in point. This is the nation's lakeland, a sort of southern

European Kashmir, but without any of the terrorism. The two key lakes are Bled and Bohinj, both cupped in the southern foothills of the Alps in a region of steep meadows and fruit orchards. They're not a million miles away from the likes of Garda and Como, but unlike their Italian relatives these clear-water enclaves have practically no development on the waterfront. There's nothing to stop you walking all the way around them, admiring the giant pike hanging like dead branches under the overhanging trees.

Bled is the better known of the two. Picture a lake with a church-crowned island at its centre, its bell tolling for a weekend wedding. A lake overlooked by a castle on a rock, a castle with butter-coloured walls and a Red Leicester roof. A lake where motor vessels are banned, and whose sculling water-boatmen belong to 20 designated local families. A lake where Austro-Hungarian emperors used to have their holidays, and where the peace is so intense you can almost hear it dripping.

Bled's tradition as a watering hole for the elite has continued right up to the present day. Marshal Tito, the architect of the former Yugoslavia, had a monumental summer house built in 13 acres of parkland on the lakeshore, and here he received the likes of Haile Selassie, Khrushchev and Indira Gandhi. Today the Vila Bled is a four-star hotel, and its functional and understated 1950s' style, with original furniture commissioned by Tito, has turned it into a trendy designer hotel almost by accident. Its clientele continues to be discreetly significant: William Hurt and Jeff Bridges were recent guests. Come here for lunch on the terrace to see if you can spot anyone familiar.

Bohinj, 20 miles west, is more remote and better suited to walkers than to resting Hollywood stars. The hills are full of waymarked trails, varying from simple lakeside circumnavigations to much more challenging mountaineering up Triglav Mountain, which at 2,864m is seriously high. Easier walking are the paths around Bohinj and up to Slap Savica, a giant waterfall which erupts from a hole midway down a huge cliff, and creates its own little vortex of wind and mist. Alternatively there's the gentler route down the Vintgar Gorge, where you look down on sipping trout from a dramatic wooden walkway fixed to the stone walls. It looks inviting, especially in the height of summer, but the water's mountain origins means that even a swift dip would render you sexually unrecognisable.

On both Bled and Bohinj there are rowing boats and Canadian canoes. For more active visitors there's canyoning and mountain guides for hire, and for the less active there are plenty of waterside restaurants where you can drink a glass of wine and read, or even write, a book.

Crime writer Agatha Christie came to Bohinj in 1967, although she didn't have a book in mind. Agatha had a horror of the press, and she and her husband Max chose Bohinj in a vain attempt to holiday somewhere where she wouldn't be recognised. Today the hotel where they stayed, the Bellevue, is a touch rundown but it still rents out Agatha's room (no 204), with antique furniture and a portrait of the author on the wall. You can sit on her balcony and gaze out at the view as she did. During the summer the hotel stages weekly Agatha Christie dinners in a library filled with memorabilia.

Unfortunately for Agatha, back in 1967, her desire to remain incognito went unheeded. The Slovenian media ran her to ground and one of the local journalists rented the room next door so that he could clamber between the balconies, clutching a bunch of flowers, like the man from Milk Tray. Agatha's husband was not happy at being thus invaded – who would be – but Agatha agreed to be interviewed.

So the journalist asked the crime writer the obvious question – was the lake going to feature in one of her books? Agatha replied, gazing out across the water, that Bohinj was 'too beautiful for a murder'.

It is, too.

PRACTICALITIES

GETTING THERE

EasyJet (☎ *0905 821 0905; www.easyjet.com*) has returns to Ljubljana (Slovenia's capital) for around £85. From Ljubljana there are regular trains (*www.slo-zeleznice.si*) to Jesenice to connect with the Bohinjska line, which has stations for Bled and Bohinj.

TOURIST INFORMATION

☎ *020 7222 5400; www.slovenia.info*

ACCOMMODATION

Hotel Bellevue $ $
By Lake Bohinj
☎ *+386 4 572 3331; www.alpinum.net*
Vila Bled $ $ $ $
Lake Bled
☎ *+386 4 579 1500; www.vila-bled.com*

23

RED SEA, WHITE SKIN, DIVE IN

MAKE A DASH FOR THE RED SEA FOR A BLAST OF
SUMMER SUN, BEFORE IT GETS TOO HOT. DIRECT
FLIGHTS HAVE TURNED SHARM EL SHEIKH INTO A
WEEKEND DESTINATION, AND WITH HOTELS NEXT TO
THE AIRPORT YOU'LL BE IN THE POOL BEFORE YOU
CAN SAY 'FLIGHTPATH'.

IN OUR ERA OF LOW-COST AIRLINES THE EMPHASIS
for weekend trips has tended to fall on cities,
culture and gastronomy, while properly sunny
winter destinations have traditionally been
week-long or fortnight-long breaks, because
they're necessarily that much further
away.

RED SEA

But now there's a way of dashing for
the sun for a long weekend that will bring
relief for anyone exhausted by the long
tunnel of January–February–March. Direct flights from British
Airways mean that you can spend as little as three nights on the
Egyptian Red Sea.

Few places are better engineered for tumbling out of the plane
and into the pool than Sharm El Sheikh. A row of upmarket hotels
line up within a towel's flick of the runway, fortunately not so busy
as to disturb hotel guests. But few visitors who tumble out of those
planes and into those hotels will realise that the land they are built
on was a war zone not so long ago. Occupied by the Israelis, it was
only handed back to Egypt in 1982.

In those days there was practically nothing here, just the sandy tip
of the inhospitable Sinai Peninsula, and the Israeli soldiers billeted
in this bleak and windy place considered it to be one of the worst
possible postings in their military careers.

But then the fighting moved away, and eventually someone realised that Sinai's astonishing marine life, its warm sea and its infallible sunshine made an irresistible combination, once you've added air conditioning and fluffy towels. Since then, the resort has had a rollercoaster ride.

Huge early growth was stalled by the tourism downturn of 9/11 and the Iraq War, during which the hotels turned to the likes of Russia and the Ukraine to fill their beds. Then came the Tony effect – ex-PM Tony Blair and family holidayed here three times during his period of office – and Sharm blossomed. Since then the resort has had its own problems with terrorist bombs, blamed on militant elements on the Sinai Peninsula, and accordingly has a heavy security presence (as does any tourist resort in Egypt these days). If you set out to explore further afield than the resort area you'll come across a massive security cordon which surrounds the whole international zone.

As it grows, Sharm is subdividing. The original town, furthest from the airport, is called the Old Market ('old' here means more than ten years) and still has a bazaar-type atmosphere, although most of its shops are aimed at tourists with the usual mix of leather poofs and plastic waterpipes. You can eat cheaply and well here for under £2 a head at the likes of the Elhusseiny Restaurant, if you're happy with Egyptian food.

Halfway back towards the airport is Na'ama Bay, the bright lights of Sharm, with a fashion store called El Rehab, and the likes of the Hard Rock Café and KFC – Kentucky Fried Camel, as the locals like to say. Families stay here in medium-range hotels, each with their own private stretch of beach. Couples and singles come here, too, for the night-time promenade, restaurants and bars.

Further back towards the airport the coast has been cultivated by the big resort hotels like the Savoy, Hyatt and Sheraton, the newest arrivals. Many have their own stretch of reef just out front, rich in coral and wonderfully exotic fish.

Beyond the airport lies the desert, with escarpments of rock that eventually conjure up mountains. Three hours from Sharm is St Catherine's Monastery, whose monks were so terrified of visitors that they sought the protection, by special decree, of the Prophet Muhammad. St Catherine's sits at the foot of Mount Sinai, where Moses received the Ten Commandments, and in many ways this part of Sinai has never lost its Biblical aspect, with camels and bedouin encampments the only human encroachment. However, coach-loads of visitors now come whirling through on day trips to the monastery, to file through the ornate church and stand by the burning bush, which turns out to be a humble bramble. The short window of visiting hours – mornings only – produces queues worse than Disney, so this is a trip better done as an overnighter, with a dawn trip up Mount Sinai, if you have the time and energy.

The bedouin hereabouts tend to drive pick-ups rather than ride camels, but they still operate independently of official government guidelines, and are readily blamed for terrorism as a result. For most tourists the usual bedu encounter will be over a delicious informal mint tea at an encampment next to a field full of what looks suspiciously like opium poppies. Best not to ask.

But the prime reason why Sharm is on the tourist map at all is the sea. In one short stride the barren land becomes fertile water, where coral, and coral-dwelling fish thrive. Every day dozens of boats set out from Sharm to a variety of snorkel and diving reefs; it's a relaxing, delightful way of fish-viewing, and especially reassuring to go in a group if you've never snorkelled before. But actually many of the hotels have fish-rich reefs of their own, so you can have a fish-viewing experience by just sauntering down to the beach.

And that's what many people do. During a three-night trip you'll have enough time to explore the resort, to visit St Catherine's Monastery and go out on a boat snorkel trip, filling the bits in between by commuting between pool, beach and bar. There are people who've been in Sharm for two weeks who never do anything more.

PRACTICALITIES

GETTING THERE

British Airways (☎ *0870 850 9850; www.ba.com*) has direct flights into Sharm El Sheikh for around £335 return.

TOURIST INFORMATION

☎ *020 7493 5283; www.gotoegypt.org*

ACCOMMODATION

The Savoy
Sharm El Sheikh $ $ $
☎ *+20 69 3 602 500; www.savoy-sharm.com*
Quite flash, with its own beach, right by the airport, but not as expensive as it looks.

PLACES OF INTEREST

St Catherine's Monastery
www.sinaimonastery.com

24

EL HIERRO, ISLAND ON THE EDGE OF THE WORLD

THE MOST REMOTE OF THE CANARY ISLANDS HAS A DECLINING POPULATION AND A SPECIES OF JURASSIC LIZARD WHICH IS A PALE SHADOW OF ITS FORMER SELF. AND YET THE STEEP, RUGGED EL HIERRO IS MORE REPRESENTATIVE OF HOW THE CANARIES ONCE WERE THAN THE OTHER ISLANDS IN A TOURIST-INFESTED ARCHIPELAGO.

ONE JANUARY, A FEW YEARS AGO, A BIZARRE STORM HIT El Hierro. Wind and rain gave the island a mohican, scouring a narrow, 1km-wide path across it. The surf mounted the western shoreline, tossed cars off the port into the sea, routed the superbly sited Parador's full-house of guests, and pounded its swimming pool to pieces. 'It was something very strange,' says the island's tourism officer, adding that a storm like that had never happened before, and they didn't think it would ever happen again. No-one was hurt, and the Parador has since reopened in exactly the same place, isolated on the shore, except now it is protected by a breakwater.

'Something very strange' is about right for El Hierro. Once upon a time, before the world was round and the Americas were just a twinkle in Christopher Columbus's eye, this was the furthest westerly point known to man. The lighthouse at its bleak western end, Faro de Ochilla, was officially the end of the world and the anchor of the zero meridian, until more of the globe was discovered and the zero was moved back to Greenwich.

Approached by ferry, El Hierro could be the world's beginning. Austere, unforgiving tan flanks rise steeply from a dark froth of lava in a steel-blue sea, past wind-contorted juniper trees bleached bone-white by the sun and into scrubland inhabited only by lizards and dust-devils. The capital, Valverde, is a one-horse town drawn across the brow of the hillside at cloud level like white beads of perspiration.

There is an almost mythical beauty here; El Hierro could even be San Borondon, the mysterious ninth Canary Island which locals claim appears out of the mist every ten–20 years. The guidebooks talk about extreme peace and picturesque poverty, but while the land is about as peaceful as the Canaries ever get – no *vamos a la playa* here – these days the poverty has receded thanks to European cash, which has been liberally applied. As a result the roads are as smooth as a baby's proverbial, in a land where smoothness doesn't come naturally. Even the fishermen have new cars; this is the European Community at work.

In the bars, however, the staple diet is still the same as it ever was: *herreño* cheese – musty and made from a mixture of goat's, sheep's and cow's milk – and pungent, urine-coloured *herreño blanco* drawn straight from the barrel.

Most of El Hierro's population lives over the top and down the other side from Valverde, in the remains of a huge volcanic crater called El Golfo, much of which has long since crumbled away into the sea. The remaining crater rim is breathtakingly wild and windy, but way down below on the crater floor the days are usually calm. Here the land is fertile, and there's even a couple of black-sand beaches.

One of El Golfo's seaside villages, Las Puntas, hosts what was once claimed to be the smallest hotel in the world, the four-room Club Puntagrande, now re-Christened the Apartamentos Punta Grande, presumably because it couldn't continue to claim hotel status; another impact of the European Community? Whichever classification it falls into, this former home of El Hierro's customs officer out on Punta Grande jetty is a very unusual place to stay. It has a bar and restaurant decorated with the roots of a huge tree, a set of rooms like a captain's bridge and a glassed conservatory right on top of the building. Its location halfway out to sea makes it look like a cross between a ship and a shed.

The European money spent on Hierro in recent years represents an attempt to halt the haemorrhaging of the population, but it is not just the human inhabitants who no longer measure up: once there were giant lizards of 1.5m long. The last specimen supposedly shuffled off his mortal coil in the 1930s and his skull rests in the British Museum, but rumours persisted for many years of sizeable lizards up in the inaccessible areas of the crater's cliffs.

Eventually 12 slightly larger than normal lizards were brought down to a new recovery centre (the 'Lagartario') by Juan Pedro Peres, man-mountain, Canarian wrestler and sometime gardener. The Lagartario has since become a tourist attraction, and so also has Juan Pedro, who continues to monitor the wild population on the cliff even though seven of his relatives lost their lives up there. The big man has a grin like a crevasse, fists like meat safes and a handshake as soft as butter, and the project biologist is plainly completely in awe of him. 'He saved my life,' he whispered. 'I had lost my grip, I was falling – and he just pinned me to the cliff with his stick.'

In their new, luxury conditions the lizards are doing well. From the original 12 there are now several hundred distributed across the island, each new generation bigger than the last, although they are still just 60cm long. Not quite the European Komodo Dragon yet, but it all adds to El Hierro's reputation as a sort of mystical, aboriginal Jurassic Park on the edge of the known world.
Even now, returning to civilisation via Tenerife after a weekend on the island, you have to shake yourself and ask – did it really exist?

PRACTICALITIES

GETTING THERE

British Airways (☎ *0870 850 9850; www.ba.com*) has direct flights into Tenerife North from £85 return. Connect with inter-island flights operated by **Binter Canarias** (☎ *+34 902 391 392; www.binternet.com*) for around £60 return.

TOURIST INFORMATION

www.elhierro.es

CAR HIRE

Cicar
www.cicar.com
At the airport. Starting price around £30 per day.
Lagartario de Guinea (Guinea Lizard Centre)
Frontera
☎ *+34 922 555 056*

ACCOMMODATION

The El Hierro Parador S S S
Las Playas
☎ *+34 922 558 036; www.parador.es*
Apartamentos Punta Grande S S
On the Embarcadero by Frontera
☎ *+34 922 559 081; www.notodohoteles.com*

25

SLEEPLESS NIGHTS ON THE LOFOTENS

WITNESS THE MIDNIGHT SUN IN NORWAY'S LOFOTEN ISLANDS, ONE OF THE FEW PLACES IN THE WORLD WHERE FISH ARE STILL PLENTIFUL. THERE'S LITTLE INCENTIVE TO GO TO BED WITH THE SUN STILL IN THE SKY. MOREOVER THIS IS THE ONLY LEISURE DESTINATION IN EUROPE WHERE YOU CAN GUARANTEE TO CATCH A COD WITH A ROD.

THE FURTHER NORTH YOU TRAVEL ACROSS NORWAY the less hospitable the landscape becomes, unless you happen to be a mosquito or a moose. By the time you reach the Arctic Circle the only houses have been banished to a thin strip of existence where the land meets the sea. This is a place of extremes, where the environment still has the upper hand; the sun barely bothers to rise in the winter, but in the summer it torments you 24 hours a day, daring you to sleep. It's a place where man is still clinging to the edge, where livelihoods are traditional, and where there's a savage beauty visible through every kitchen window.

The mainstay of most of these shore-bound Norwegian communities is fishing, and by staying out of Europe the country has managed to protect its fish stocks from foreigners – apart from those who come here on holiday.

The focus of both fishing and holidaymaking hereabouts is the stunningly beautiful Lofoten Islands, which lie just offshore from the mainland town of Bodø. This is one of the few places left in the world which still has a real miracle of a marine harvest every year.

The Lofotens are as pristine as they were 10,000 years ago, when the Ice Age withdrew. The five islands rear dramatically out of an aquamarine sea, through a thin skirt of green up to steely mountains which look far higher than they really are.

But don't assume that just because the Lofotens are north of the Arctic Circle that they are raw, wind-ravaged places. The season of fruitfulness may be short here but from mid May the ground bursts with wild flowers and berries, the skies fill with cuckoos, curlews and eagles, and the water churns with migrating cod and salmon. When the sun shines there's a clarity in the air which almost defies description, piercing water so pure that you can watch the starfish grazing, 30ft down.

And then, of course, for about six weeks right in the middle of the year, there's the midnight sun. All lighthouses in Lofoten are switched off from 30 April and not turned back on until 6 August, when the sun finally decides to lie down.

It is an odd feeling, daylight when there should be night. You draw your curtains and go to bed in the knowledge that the sun is still rolling along the horizon like a billiard ball. Its presence is a challenge. 'What are you, man or mouse? Bedtime, pah!' So of course you get up again.

A good place to have a closer look is Eggum, on the Atlantic side of the island chain. Here, at two o'clock in the morning, the air is heavy with silence and the seagulls move at a quarter speed. Here the lazy orb – can't be arsed to go to bed, nor to climb properly into the sky – plays sweet nothings, creating pools of light on a shifting mercury sea stitched with skerries.

Inevitably, in a place this far north, the weather is a key factor in determining what you do. It's one of those destinations where, if the day is nice enough to make you think of doing something, you should do it straightaway before the opportunity goes.

In fine conditions there's excellent walking on a network of inland tracks that climb past peat-dark lakes through cloudberries, saxifrage and reindeer moss, with eagles above and the occasional moose up ahead. There are coast paths, too, winding through dwarf willow and mountain ash to ruined villages.

In less good weather there's always the fishing. A Klondike-like atmosphere descends on the Lofotens in the early months of the year, when the cod come to breed in the Vestfjord. Some 50,000 tons are landed in a few short weeks, a flurry of activity which in itself is enough to keep the island economy afloat. Hundreds of thousands of fish are put out on huge drying frames all over the islands, and ultimately exported to Italy and Spain where they form the basis of salt-cod cuisine.

Tourism arrived here almost as a by-product, because once the cod season is over, the fishermen have time – and the best months of the year – on their hands. They also have large numbers of *rorbu*, or fishermen's cabins, right at the water's edge. Many of these cabins have their own rowing boats, and every corner shop has fishing gear.

If you'd prefer a skipper to show you how, the more attractive settlements – Henningsvaer, Nusfjord, Reine and Å – offer boat trips with fishing, but the best scenery/cod combination is out of Svolvær, the commercial capital, from where boats travel up to the Trollfjord, a dramatically narrow sheer-sided inlet, with cod-catching and eagle-feeding on the way.

Back on land, wooden churches make the biggest architectural statements in this landscape, with big barn-like interiors where fishermen give thanks for staying alive. The huge fish-drying racks run them a close second, architecturally speaking, and on a sombre day you could mistake them, too, for giant, arched cathedrals to cod.

There's one word that appears with puzzling frequency in both churches and graveyards: *fred*, meaning 'peace'. In the Lofotens, there's an awful lot of *fred* about.

PRACTICALITIES

GETTING THERE

SAS Braathens (☎ +47 91 50 54 00; *www.sasbraathens.no*) flies from London via Oslo to Bodø from £310 return. Onward short flights across from Bodø to Lofoten with **Wideroe** (☎ +47 81 00 12 00; *www.wideroe.no*) from £50 return.

TOURIST INFORMATION

The **Lofoten Tourist Board**
Svolvaer
☎ +47 76 06 98 00; *www.lofoten-tourist.no*

CAR HIRE

Car hire is expensive on the island. **Hertz** (☎ 0870 599 6699; *www.hertz.co.uk*) charges start from around £55/day.

ACCOMMODATION

Reine Rorbuer `S S S`
Reine
☎ +47 76 09 22 22; *www.reinerorbuer.no*
Original but updated turf-roofed cabins in one of the Lofotens' most scenically located towns.

SUMMER

Summer has arrived and suddenly everything is possible in the British countryside, which is why there are six suggestions in this HOME FRONT, kicking off with letterboxing on Dartmoor, a sort of orienteering treasure-hunt. Then there's tipi camping in Cornwall, to awaken your inner child. Still in Cornwall, I'm recommending an old-fashioned nautical adventure to be had out of the small bay at St Mawes. Or else you could head over to Dorset for a taste of what England's southern shore would have really been like if we hadn't built bungalows all along it. Elsewhere, there's the Welsh town famous for bog-snorkelling and real-ale wobbling, and the handsome West Highland Railway Line famous for movie making and for the only remaining proper working steam train in the UK. (HOME FRONT 26–31)

Over in Europe, I'm avoiding honeypot summer destinations. In Austria, the Danube city of Linz has a great street festival in late July. In northern Germany, 'hay-hotel' rural cycle routes lead from one farmer's barn to the next. In Sweden, there's a truly adventurous mix of cycle-trolleying and camping-canoeing in the land of the moose and the mosquito. In Spain there's the chance to get all spiritual in Galicia, scenic home to Europe's freshest and cheapest fish cuisine. And in Hamburg you can rise at dawn on a Sunday morning to party in a fish market and be abused by an eel-monger; a surprisingly pleasurable experience. (MEDIUM DISTANT 32–37)

With so much going on in the UK and Europe in summer, you don't need to venture further afield. The only distant weekend I've included in this season is a trip to the northern Syrian city of Aleppo, to a tunnel-like souk like something out of Indiana Jones in the land of the Crusaders. (FURTHER FLUNG 38)

PRICE GRADING FOR ACCOMMODATION

$ – up to £40 for a double room; $$ – £40–70 double; $$$ – £70–110 double; $$$$ – £110 + double.

DESTINATIONS

HOME FRONT

MEDIUM DISTANT

FURTHER FLUNG

26

Hunt the Dartmoor Letterboxes

LETTERBOXING IS A QUIRKY, YEAR-ROUND TREASURE HUNT WITH A LONG TRADITION. THE IDEA IS TO USE A COMPASS AND MAP TO FIND SOME 2,000 'LETTERBOXES' HIDDEN OVER THE FACE OF DARTMOOR. DEDICATION, APPLICATION AND AN AIR OF ECCENTRICITY REQUIRED.

THIS WIDE, BLEAK EXPANSE OF DEVONSHIRE MOORLAND is traditionally known for its high-security prison, its wild ponies, its military survival exercises and its Baskerville Hounds. But every year some 10,000 people stride out into its remoter corners with none of the above in mind. Instead they're focused on a strange kind of treasure hunt: they're out letterboxing.

Dartmoor's letterboxes are not bright red and they don't stand out for miles. On the contrary, they are as near as dammit invisible, and you could easily stand on top of one without knowing it's there.

For participants, these letterboxes are at the centre of an elaborate, long-winded game. The boxes themselves – around 2,000 of them – are the sort of dull grey plastic tubs you might see on the shelves of a pharmacy, and they have been carefully hidden in natural cavities all over the surface of the 365-square-mile moor. Each contains a tailor-made rubber stamp, a visitor's book, and the hider's contact for any problems.

The hiders then publish clues – usually compass bearings, together with a brief topographical description of the hiding place, viz 'under a triangular rock 20 paces east of a willow clump' – either in the letterboxers' monthly newsletter, or in the annual catalogue.

Then the hunters sally forth. Each carries a distinctive calling-card rubber stamp of their own, and they leave their marks in the visitor's books of the boxes they find, at the same time as taking an impression of the box's resident stamp for their own collection. They also sometimes leave items of post for the next finder to take back to civilisation, for posting in the normal way, thus earning the 'letterbox' description.

If it all sounds fairly mad, then that's because it is. Only the British would create a sort of fox-hunting without tears, cross-fertilising the satisfaction of trainspotting with the skills of orienteering.

The activity dates back to 1854, when one James Perrott left a glass jar by a remote pool so that visitors could leave their calling cards to show they'd been there. It was revived about 30 years ago by Godfrey Swinscow, who still runs the 100 Club for people who've collected the stamps of more than 100 boxes (12,800 members and climbing). In those days Godfrey was so keen, he was prepared to do anything for a box. He once found a carrier bag hanging on his car's wing mirror containing a clue which required him to put on a dress and skip through the woods singing 'I believe in fairies' to find the box in question. The photos came through the post a couple of days later.

Letterboxing's current proponents attribute its continuing popularity to the fact that it costs practically nothing to do and placates the primitive need to hunt and gather, but 'without stealing any birds' eggs'. It wasn't, however, always sanctioned by the Moor's owners, the National Trust, who didn't like the way it encouraged tugging at tussocks and ferreting around in the roots of trees whose hold on life was already tenuous. Not to mention the distribution of very non-biodegradable lumps of plastic over an otherwise pristine environment.

These days, however, the relationship is more harmonious. In fact the letterboxing veterans know the moor so well that they are sometimes called on to help with search and rescue operations.

Letterboxers don't wear any particular uniform, but are readily identifiable through their hand-bearing compasses, 1:25,000 Ordnance Survey maps, stout boots and slight air of eccentricity. On a good weekend there could be up to 1,000 of them out puzzling over clues and fossicking under hawthorns, rocks and standing stones. Draw near, and you can hear them squinting at the peaks and declaiming their bearings like bomber command. 'South Hessary 225 degrees. North five points and climb.' Then, moments later, checking again. 'That's it. 095 on the Nutcracker. We should be right on top of it.' Bombs away.

Although there's no official committee, letterboxers tend to meet twice annually on clock-change days in a village hall on the Moor. Mind you, these days the internet is a favoured method for gossip and exchange of information.

If you're going to try your hand at letterboxing, you'll want to stay somewhere local and picturesque, in a village like North Bovey, 20 miles west of Exeter. Here the Ring of Bells is pretty much the quintessential country pub with rooms, being thatched, 13th century and with an original chimney oven where the village bread was baked. The pub is plain and unschmaltzed with the floors all wonky and the beams low enough for brain surgery, but that didn't stop it nearly going bust during the Foot and Mouth crisis.

It was, in fact, saved by a dozen forty-something friends who'd all graduated from Bristol University, and who used to come down here for weekends of beer, laughter and divot-creation. When they heard the Ring of Bells was about to go under, they clubbed together and bought the place. It seems that several of them were looking for a way through their mid-life crises, and a country pub offered a tempting prospect – the chance to spend the rest of their working lives down the pub.

It was fun while it lasted. The group of friends has since sold up, and are back concentrating on their more mainstream careers. The Ring of Bells is very much back on track.

GETTING THERE

Dartmoor sits between the A30 and the A38 west of Exeter. Best railway access (*www.nationalrail.co.uk*) is via Totnes.

TOURIST INFORMATION

Dartmoor

↘ *01626 832093; www.dartmoor-npa.gov.uk*

ACCOMMODATION

Ring of Bells Inn $ $ $
North Bovey
↘ *01647 440375; www.ringofbellsinn.com*

LETTERBOXING

The catalogue of registered **Letterboxes** (£6 with 75p postage) is available from Tony Moore (*25 Sanderspool Cross, South Brent, Devon TQ10 9LR;*
↘ *01364 73414*).

There's an official website (*www.letterboxingondartmoor.co.uk*), and one less official (*www.dartmoorletterboxing.org*).

Dartmoor National Park (DNPA) produces its own guide, *Letterboxing with Moor Care and Less Wear*, which is available from all DNPA information centres.

27
CORNWALL'S PALEFACE ENCAMPMENT

RENT A TIPI IN CORNWALL. IN AN OVERGROWN
QUARRY WITH A SECRET LAKE WHERE FISH VIRTUALLY
JUMP INTO YOUR ROWING BOAT. IF YOU HAVEN'T GOT
CHILDREN OF YOUR OWN, THEN MAYBE THIS IS THE
TIME TO BORROW SOME.

ON A RECENT SUMMER'S EVE A FATHER WAS SEATED
outside his tipi in the gloaming of a forest
clearing, the last of his family's hand-caught
rainbow trout still baking in the fire pit beside
him. Murmuring from within the tipi was his son
Buffalo Dreaming (more commonly known to his
mother as Thomas) rehearsing his sleepy younger
sister Peach Blossom (her mother knows her as
Rhena) in the names of the Chosen Ones. 'Yoda,' he
said. 'Odour,' she repeated. 'Yarael Poof,' said he,
'aerial poo,' said she. 'Deepa Billaba...'. And so the
litany progressed as the last droplet of liquid sun
buried itself in Mother Earth and the stars popped
out overhead.

It was an incantation that could so easily have belonged to a
Native American reservation in deepest Arizona, except that this
wasn't America, but deepest Cornwall, and the names were not
those of war-painted ancestors, but of the Jedi Council; Buffalo
Dreaming had just watched *The Phantom Menace* for the nth time
on DVD and wanted to make sure his sister was up to speed. Mind
you, the tipi itself was so well hidden that it might as well have been
on another planet; certainly ordinary mortal mobile phones found
no network they could recognise.

The tipi in question belonged to a substantial encampment in
Tregildrens Quarry in mid Cornwall, close to Port Isaac, and within

15 minutes' drive of Boscastle and Tintagel. Just down the coast to the west are Rock and Padstow (aka Padstein, thanks to the burgeoning empire of seafood chef Rick Stein), both locations where the truly posh have their holiday homes and where Harry and Wills had their hols.

A tipi, however, is something different in a world increasingly full of boutique hotels. Now that tents have transmogrified themselves into plastic bungalows in suburban encampments that come complete with leisure centres and supermarkets, much of the old magic has gone out of mainstream camping. Remember the camping of old? Those happy weeks of being damp and smelly, eating Vesta just-add-water curry and carefully rotating – but not washing – your socks? The success of tipi encampments like this one in Cornwall (there are others in Wales, the Lake District, Norfolk, Northumberland and probably several more places I don't yet know about) indicates that there's still a demand for a more authentic camping experience in the semi-wild, and you don't have to be a hippy-trippy Obe Kenobi to enjoy it.

Tregildrens's location means that this is far enough west to feel properly Cornish on a weekend visit, but not so far into Cornwall that you get completely entangled in the nightmare of summertime holiday traffic. Mind you, finding the actual site is not easy; the lane that runs past is car-flagellatingly narrow, and bears no signs of anything remotely tipi-ish, although if you reach a cottage called Nomansland, you've gone too far.

The quarry itself is barely recognisable as a quarry at all now that it is so overgrown. Rather it looks like a densely wooded valley, interrupted by the occasional grassy path leading to where the tipis stand, like hooded giants, in their own private clearings. Look hard and you might spot a portaloo lurking in the bushes; brush aside a branch and you could find a tap sprouting from a tree. Only ethereal spirit voices betwixt birch and oak suggest that other tipi-dwellers are in the vicinity.

Once you've unlaced the entrance-way, you'll find a tipi's interior pretty spacious, the floors strewn with colourful mats, the lodge poles hung with a selection of ornate and practical lanterns. The poles come together at a point of winking sky about 18ft above the ground, a hole that keeps the tipi ventilated on a baking summer's day, when more conventional canvas gets hot enough to stew one's fruit. Closing that hole at night requires a bit of pole-management, a quickly learned skill.

All in all it is the basis for a romantic, fairytale weekend, although not everything is to everyone's liking. During his stay, the father of Buffalo Dreaming and Peach Blossom spoke to a mother and daughter who were leaving early to go back to Birmingham, because of undue mole molestation. It seems moles had come up under their tipi at night and pushed their possessions around from beneath the groundsheet; it was hard to suppress a smile.

Anyway, Buffalo Dreaming and Peach Blossom had no inhibitions about the wildlife. They'd spent the day splashing about in the clear waters of the subterranean stream-fed lake, which apparently reaches depths of 70ft at the cliffy end. Dragonflies skimmed the surface and large rainbow trout patrolled below, unbothered by paleface thrashing. The fish didn't even seem too bothered later, when four of their number went thrashing unwillingly to the surface assisted by the same palefaces, who were now equipped with rod, line and Mother's Pride.

So it was, having caught our dinner, we returned to our clearing to prepare the cooking fire and let the evening commence, which is where you found us at the beginning of this piece. Sans TV, sans microwave dinners and sans Windows Vista. Mind you, Peach Blossom is happy wherever there are Jammy Dodgers, and Buffalo Dreaming had *Star Wars* on his mind.

Cornwall's paleface encampment

PRACTICALITIES

GETTING THERE

Tregildrens Quarry is halfway between St Kew and Pendoggent, north of Wadebridge just off the A39. Nearest railway station Bodmin Parkway (*www.nationalrail.co.uk*).

TOURIST INFORMATION

Cornwall

❱ *01872 322900; www.visitcornwall.co.uk*

ACCOMMODATION

Cornish Tipi Holidays $ $

❱ *01208 880781; www.Cornish-tipi-holidays.co.uk*

You can choose between solo tipis in their own enclosures, or a group of tipis in a small tipi village.

DORSET'S BUNGALOW-FREE SHORE

28

THE ENGLISH COAST IS NOT NORMALLY NOTED FOR ITS WILDERNESS EXPERIENCES. BUT THERE IS ONE SLICE OF SHORE WHERE YOUR MOBILE PHONE WILL STRUGGLE, WHERE A WHOLE VILLAGE HAS BEEN ABANDONED AND WHERE BUNGALOW BUILDERS HAVE YET TO GET A FOOT IN THE DOOR.

IT'S SUMMER AND THE BRITISH SEASIDE HAS COME TO town. All along the south coast the deckchair attendants are ready with their tickets and the end-of-the-pier performers have prepared their lines. The resorts are having a last-minute primp in the hope of attracting sufficient money to carry them through the year.

There is, however, one stretch of shore which holds itself aloof, the stretch between Swanage and Weymouth. This section of the Jurassic Coast is remarkably wild, rearing up like a primeval beast and shaking off all attempts to urbanise. The so-called Isle of Purbeck has no road along its shore; Cretaceous landforms and unexploded ordnance make sure of that.

DORSET COAST

The wildness begins at Old Harry Rocks, also the beginning of the South West Coast Path, and it's an auspicious beginning: the rocks are actually chalk stacks and cliffs, counterparts to the Isle of Wight's Needles visible across the water. It's worth walking out here on a sunny morning, when the low sun touches up Old Harry's complexion, almost making him look young again. You can stand on the sward (famous for rare butterflies) to watch the ships rounding the point for Poole Harbour, but beware the sudden cliff edge, however; Old Harry gives the finger to Health and Safety, so this is a place to stare at mortality and think about God. Or you could head a

bit north and stare at the Studland nudist beach and think about the ageing process instead.

Swanage itself is an odd place. Part Victorian resort, part retirement home, part sanctuary for alternative lifestylers, it has a classic sandy beach with a classically ugly 1960s' arts centre halfway along it, like a decaying school science block. Its pier is run by a trust which makes a charge (40p) for 'strolling', and has an interesting line in brass plaques nailed to the boards, with inscriptions like 'David and Judith, we made it! June 2000'.

In town, you'll find the unashamedly kitsch Candle World, full of scent and glitter; Rainbow's End, a humorous, hippy-chic boutique (T-shirts with messages like 'I want it all and I want it covered in chocolate') and an intriguing café called Earthlights in a chapel-like building built by Thomas Hardy's apprentice, during the latter's days as a church architect. Earthlights seems to be a centre for sorcery and witchcraft, the place to buy your copy of *Kindred Spirit* magazine and have your Tarot done. Or just a cracking good bowl of soup.

Swanage doesn't really feature on the list of British resorts, despite the pier. The town really grew up around another kind of industry altogether, one of stone. To seek it out, head uphill out of town towards villages like Langton and Worth Matravers, where walls and houses seem to grow organically out of weathered rock.

The Romans were the first to quarry here, and 12th–14th-century cathedrals such as Salisbury and Exeter all contain Purbeck stone. Even today Purbeck is still home to one-man-and-his-dad limestone quarries which welcome passing customers, and a couple of them have made some remarkable prehistoric discoveries during their day jobs. The affable John Keats at Keats's Quarry, just off the Worth to Langton Road, might spare a minute or two to tell you about the dinosaur footprints he found.

Even if you don't rock-hop around a few quarries, be sure to spend some time at the wonderfully unreconstructed stonecutters' pub the Square & Compass in Worth Matravers. Its front garden is filled with a charivari of fossil and rock, while beer is served from a hatch inside, with photos of former quarrymen lining the walls. This is a particularly good place to start or finish a walk along the coastal path, which runs along the top of significantly high cliffs. Popular tradition has it that Napoleon was rowed ashore somewhere on this stretch, looked up at the cliffs and decided that invading England would be too much of a tall order.

There's a sturdy, lonely 800-year-old chapel on St Aldhelm's Head, and to its east another former quarry with the lively name Dancing Ledge, cut right into the sea cliffs. The Ledge comes complete with a hand-carved swimming pool, filled by the tide, where the quarrymen would wash off the heat and the dust before walking home.

The swirling hills and large feudal farming estates continue around Kimmeridge, practically the only village which dares put a feeler out to the shore. And between here and Lulworth Cove (a major summer attraction and therefore probably to be avoided) stretches a huge swathe of land dedicated to warfare: the 2,830ha Lulworth firing range, a practice ground for tanks and artillery. The coastal path continues blithely on, but a rigorously maintained flag system, illustrated with smoking boots, tells walkers whether or not it is safe to proceed.

There is, in fact, one last village right in the middle of this pseudo war-zone. It's called Tyneham, and its villagers were forced to abandon it to the MOD during World War II, although the compulsory purchase orders didn't come through until the 1960s. Visitable on non-firing days, Tyneham is a rather moving experience. In the tiny school there are still pegs with children's names chalked beneath them, and a sign on the church door reads 'Please treat our village kindly. We will be back'. They weren't.

PRACTICALITIES

GETTING THERE

Purbeck lies south of the A352 to the west of Bournemouth. The nearest railway station is Wareham (*www.nationalrail.co.uk*).

TOURIST INFORMATION

Swanage

✆ *01929 422885; www.visitsouthwest.co.uk, www.jurassiccoast.com*

ACCOMMODATION

Kimmeridge Farm House $ $

Kimmeridge

✆ *01929 480990; www.kimmeridgefarmhouse.co.uk*

High-quality B&B.

Dorset Coastal Cottages $ $ $

✆ *0800 980 4070; www.dorsetcoastalcottages.com*

Properties – see Elisabeth's Cottage in Kimmeridge – for weekend rental.

PLACES OF INTEREST

For more information on quarrying, go to *www.purbeckstone.co.uk*.
For access to Tyneham across the firing range see the opening dates on *www.purbeck.gov.uk/default.aspx?page=7652*.

BOG-TASTIC
LLANWRTYD WELLS

29

COME TO LLANWRTYD WELLS AND GET MUD IN YOUR
SNEAKERS. THIS MID-WALESIAN TOWN HAS A HIGHLY
UNUSUAL CALENDAR OF EVENTS, INCLUDING WORLD
CHAMPIONSHIP BOG-SNORKELLING, AND ITS CLOSE
RELATIVE WORLD CHAMPIONSHIP MOUNTAIN-BIKE
BOG-SNORKELLING.

ESTATE AGENTS ARE NOTORIOUSLY GLIB ON MOST
subjects, but amongst the few things likely to
render them speechless – momentarily at least –
is the query: 'and what has the bog-snorkelling
done for property prices?' In most parts of the
country such a question would be straight out of *Mr
Bean Gets a Mortgage*, but in the smallest town in
Britain it is a perfectly reasonable enquiry. And like as
not the response will be that, yes, the bog-snorkelling
has been pretty helpful. Bog-tastically so.

LLANWRTYD
WELLS

In fact, without the bog-snorkelling – or the forest-
morrissing and real-ale wobbling, for that matter –
there's a strong possibility that you'd have missed
out on Llanwrtyd Wells (population 604) altogether. To the motorist in
a hurry, this mid-Walesian town isn't much more than a river bridge,
petrol station and public WC on the A483. But for anyone with a taste
for the unusual it offers rather more, as well as one of only two
Michelin-starred restaurants in Wales.

Llanwrtyd Wells isn't particularly old, nor is it architecturally much
more than bog-standard. However it sits in beguiling countryside on
the banks of the river Irfon, at the centre of one of the few remaining
wildernesses in the United Kingdom: the Cambrian Mountains. It is
those mountains which initially put the town on the map, and which
have given it a second and third chance at life.

In its first manifestation, Llanwrtyd was, as the 'Wells' part of its name suggests, a spa. There were – and are, albeit now disused – three main volcanic springs, one rich in magnesium, one in sulphur and one in iron. This combination of fresh air and health-enhancing waters encouraged miners from the Valleys to jump on the train in Swansea and trundle north to Llanwrtyd for their summer holidays.

Many of the downtown properties were built as large Victorian guesthouses to accommodate this annual influx of trade. The miners usually brought their own food, which would be cooked for them by the guesthouse owners, while they themselves would do a daily circuit of watering hole, chapel, and choir concert in the town halls. The unofficial Welsh national anthem, *Sospan Fach*, was composed here.

By the 1930s, however, business was dwindling fast, and by the 1950s Llanwrtyd was a ghost town. Agreeing that something must be done, the farmers pooled their farm ponies and created the first pony-trekking association in Wales. Not only did this bring back visitors and revenue, but it also brought floods of young ladies who loved horses and showed a healthy interest in strapping stableyard lads.

Accordingly, the trekker era refreshed parts of the community which other activities did not reach. 'We had one old chap, Dai, who must have been in his seventies, but he was a terrible flirt with the girls,' recalls former headmaster Bryn Davies. 'There's one story of him offering to share his orange with one of a new group on their first day. "Ooh, no, I couldn't, Dai, oranges is for when you're pregnant," giggles the girl. "In that case I'll let you have some at the end of the week," replies Dai, with a twinkle in his eye.'

In 1975, the trekking business was still sufficiently thriving to encourage energetic Manchester-born Gordon Green to invest in the Neuadd Arms, the town's central hotel, but his timing was bad. A couple of years later trekker numbers were diminishing, but Green still had a hungry hotel to fill. He decided that Llanwrtyd needed some new, headline-grabbing attractions.

His first idea was the Man versus Horse Marathon, a 22-mile race run over all sorts of terrain, now in its 25th year. It was instantly successful, and these days attracts around 35 horses and 350 runners (so far a horse has always won, but the margin over the first runner home is down to 90 seconds). Spurred on by this success, late-night discussions over the bar of the Neuadd produced a string of further initiatives, most of them walking, running and mountain-bike based, usually with an eccentric twist, such as the free beer at checkpoints on the Real Ale Wobble cycle race.

These initiatives today produce a throughput of around 25,000 visitors – outnumbering the local population by 40 to 1. The most headline-grabbing of all is the bog-snorkelling, the 'dirtiest sport in Britain', the product of a bar-room think-tank the exact details of which are still hazy, thanks to the lateness of the night and the wobble factor in the ale. By contrast, one of the biggest in terms of entries is Morris in the Forest, an annual get-together of Morris dancers from all over the British Isles, with workshops and a nine-mile dance-walk through bog-free (and ale-free) woodland.

These and the other 20-odd events which comprise Llanwrtyd's unusual calendar have helped to resuscitate the community. In the mid 1970s the roll of the local school had declined to just 30; 20 years later it peaked at 128. A town that could have vanished is still very much on its feet.

Meanwhile the man who started the regeneration has retired from the hotel business to a bungalow he had built on a hill just outside the village, from where he can watch the red kites skim over the fields. He may be in his seventies, but he's still messily involved, preparing the bog for its annual invasion. 'Somehow I always end up with that particular short straw,' he says, ruefully. 'In all these years I've not yet managed to do any actual snorkelling, but there's at least one pair of my glasses in there.'

PRACTICALITIES

GETTING THERE

Llanwrtyd is on the A483 west of Builth Wells and lies on the scenic Heart of Wales railway line that links Swansea to Shrewsbury (*www.nationalrail.co.uk*).

TOURIST INFORMATION

Llanwrtyd

↳ *01591 610666; www.visitwales.co.uk*

ACCOMMODATION

Neuadd Arms Hotel $ $
Llanwrtyd
↳ *01591 610236; www.neuaddarmshotel.co.uk*
Comfortable, characterful and central.

EVENTS

The Llanwrtyd roster of activities is organised by **Green Events**. See the calendar on *http://llanwrtyd-wells.powys.org.uk*.

30

STEAMING THROUGH THE WEST HIGHLANDS

TAKE THE STEAM TRAIN OUT TO THE WESTERNMOST POINT IN SCOTLAND, WHOSE WONDERFULLY CLEAN SANDY BEACHES WERE THE BACKDROP TO BILL FORSYTH'S *LOCAL HERO*. THE VIEW FROM THE WINDOW OF THE *JACOBITE* – WHICH ITSELF RECENTLY PLAYED THE PART OF HARRY POTTER'S *HOGWART'S EXPRESS* – IS BETTER THAN ANY MOVIE.

IF YOU'VE NEVER BEEN TO THE WEST HIGHLANDS OF Scotland, then shame on you. You've missed some of the loveliest landscapes in all of Britain. A mix of mountain and pasture, loch and sea, beach and island, with bits of stirring history thrown in.

During the summer months this best of Scotland is best seen from the only scheduled train on the British railway network which is still pulled by a steam locomotive, the *Jacobite*, which works the West Highland Line, from Fort William to Mallaig.

And what a setting for it: the line picks its way through some of Scotland's most grand and gaunt scenery. To the south lies Moidart and the Ardnamurchan peninsula, to the north the wilderness of Knoydart (also a peninsula but accessible only by boat); to the east rise the brute shoulders of Ben Nevis, Britain's highest mountain, and to the west the Inner Hebrides obscure the horizon. The train weaves past all this, running along the edge of lochs, through woodland and broaching the pristine sandy bays where *Local Hero* was filmed. Far better than travelling by the road which shadows it, which has parts that will require your full attention if you want to stay alive.

The train's name derives from a crucial moment in Scottish history, when Bonnie Prince Charlie, leader of the Jacobite rebellion and so nearly king of all Scotland and England, raised his standard for the first time, beginning a campaign which took him to within striking distance of London. His final defeat at Culloden was the beginning of the end for the old Highland chiefs and clan system.

Prince Charlie's monument stands at Glenfinnan, on the northern tip of steeply glaciated Loch Shiel. The monument is walking distance from Glenfinnan station, the *Jacobite*'s first stop, but it can be better viewed from the decks of a stately old boat which runs daily wildlife cruises down the loch; three of Scotland's 40-something breeding pairs of golden eagles nest in these lochside mountains. If you look back from the boat decks towards the monument, then you'll see behind it the multi-spanned viaduct that had its big cinematic moment in *Harry Potter and the Chamber of Secrets*. This is the one where Harry and Ron chased the train in their flying Ford Anglia, with the *Jacobite* playing the part of the *Hogwart's Express*. It also provided good temporary employment for a local rugby player who looks remarkably like Robbie Coltrane.

Glenfinnan station itself has a small and fairly eccentric museum about the history of the line, as well as a nicely upholstered dining-car café and an old railway sleeping car which offers honest accommodation to passing walkers. This is definitely the place to stay if you don't mind relatively primitive arrangements. But if you're continuing onwards on the *Jacobite*, then don't stray too far from the station; it lingers here for around 25 minutes, but after that it won't wait.

Apart from its end destination, the fishing and ferry harbour at Mallaig, the *Jacobite*'s only other stop, by request, is Arisaig, the westernmost station in Britain. Views here are of sea, sky, and the so-called Cocktail Isles of Rum, Eigg and Muck, reached by boat both from Mallaig (all year) and from Arisaig (summer time only). A journey out to these islands is a visually and sociologically stimulating experience, although it'll take you considerably longer than a weekend if you want to spend any time on them.

In Arisaig itself an exhibition in the community-run Land, Sea and Island Centre reveals how this was the departure port for the Hebrides until the quay was finally built at Mallaig. There's also a touching note from Peter Capaldi, one of the stars of *Local Hero*, to the effect that filming in Arisaig 'was a pivotal experience in my life'. Nearby Camusdarach Beach, with immaculate silver sand and deep-blue sea, was one of the settings for the film and represents a surprising touch of the Caribbean in Scotland; at least it does until you step into the water.

The Arisaig exhibition also reveals how this corner of Scotland was the training ground for World War II's Special Operations Executive, preparing the men and women who were to be dropped in behind enemy lines. The SOE requisitioned elegant Arisaig House (now the nucleus of a clutch of holiday rental cottages) and used the West Highland Line to practise driving locomotives, falling off trains and blowing up the track. Back then it was a deadly serious business; fortunately these days it's just the stuff of movies.

The last stop of the route, beyond Morar (whose loch is supposed to be home to Morag, a close relative of Nessie) is Mallaig, the end of the line and port for the Isles. This is a proper fishing and ferry port, and too busy, in its own small way, to be bothered with romance. There'll probably be a seal in the harbour, ice on the move and fish boxes in the market hall. Best thing to do here is to spectate for a while and then adjourn to the café in the Seaman's Mission for a very good-value cup of tea and home baking, to contemplate your next move. You've an hour-and-a-half here before the *Jacobite* goes back again.

PRACTICALITIES

GETTING THERE

The West Highland Line (*www.nationalrail.co.uk*) runs from Fort William to Mallaig, and is shadowed by the A830 all the way.

TOURIST INFORMATION

Fort William

☎ *08452 255121; www.visithighlands.com*

The unofficial *www.road-to-the-isles.org.uk* is also very good, and has details of Arisaig's Land, Sea and Island Centre.

ACCOMMODATION

The Glenfinnan Sleeping Car S

Glenfinnan station

☎ *01397 722300*

Leven House S S

☎ *01687 450238; www.thelevenhouse.co.uk*

Quality B&B accommodation near Arisaig.

TRAINS

The *Jacobite Express* (☎ *01524 737751; www.steamtrain.info*) runs daily between Fort William and Mallaig between May and October. Return fares £28 adult, £16 child.

31

UP THE CREEK WITH *EVE*

A WEEKEND SAIL ON THE *EVE OF ST MAWES*, A
REPLICA PILOT CUTTER BASED AT ST MAWES IN
SOUTHERN CORNWALL. EXCELLENT FOOD AND
EQUALLY EXCELLENT SMALL-SCALE ADVENTURES,
DODGING IN AND OUT OF BAYS AND ESTUARIES. YOU
DON'T EVEN HAVE TO KNOW WHAT YOU'RE DOING.

SERIOUS SAILING BOATS FALL INTO TWO CAMPS. THE ALL-singing, all-dancing carbon-fibre, winch and wire variety, where, to be honest, one person could practically do everything and the passengers just come along to mix the gin. Or classic boats, where sailing is all bump and grind, where even short journeys quickly achieve legendary status and where every inch sailed into the wind is hard earned.

SOUTHERN
CORNWALL

Eve of St Mawes belongs to the salty-tales boats-with-bowsprits variety. In full flight she carries five sails, with nary a winch in sight, but plenty of rigging on which to dry your socks (although the first rule of sailing is that things don't get dry, they just get less moist).

Eve's hemp is there to be hauled, and it takes some hauling, but once she's set, she's the stuff of picture postcards. The reward for hemp-blistered hands lies in surging past coastal car parks under buxom sail and watching even the snoggers break apart to stare.

Hewn out of oak, mahogany and larch, with a mast made out of Douglas fir, *Eve* is modelled on a Bristol Channel pilot cutter from the 1890s, the boating world's equivalent of an old Bentley – handsome, heavy and a brute to coax around corners. And her beat – a Cornish coastline attacked by God's chainsaw – has plenty of corners in it.

Up the creek with *Eve*

Eve's base at St Mawes is part of the wider Fal Estuary, a sort of less-intensively sailed Solent but without the ships, the smell and the snobbery. Over at Falmouth itself (there's a foot ferry across) is the new National Maritime Museum Cornwall, which has a big wind tank with radio-controlled sailing boats where you can get to grips with the concept of tacking without getting wet. If you are one of those people who think that 'single-handed' Ellen MacArthur is short of an arm or two, then it may be an idea to come here before you actually step on a sailing boat.

Eve's annual programme involves loitering with intent around Cornish creeks and cliffs, with the choice of water depending on the prevailing wind. The British weather usually gives the crew plenty to talk about – and the opportunity to see if you can honk and pee at the same time – but a skipper on a short break is unlikely to push hard into foul conditions.

For most trips the emphasis is on exploring, whether it be on sea or on land. So, for example, a day that starts with the intention of heading east from St Mawes to Fowey could see a complete change of plan after a couple of hours of upwind bashing; by lunchtime you could be ghosting up the Helford River towards Daphne du Maurier's *Frenchman's Creek*, where the only sound is the twitter of birds and the gurgle of the tide under the stem. Until, that is, you let fly the anchor and the chain growls and chatters like a castle full of ghosts. The smugglers who once lived along these riverbanks have long since been replaced by millionaires.

After lunch, while the sea is raging and head-butting the headlands at having lost you, you'll be covering good mileage on the coast path between banks of campion, ragwort and wild garlic, returning to the boat well exercised and well ready for a New Zealand Chardonnay and a haddock kedgeree. And that night you'll slip ashore again across a carpet of phosphoresence under a waxing moon, to go to the pub.

Over a pint or two the skipper will probably tell you about the shipyard upriver at the village of Gweek, where *Eve* was actually built back in 1997. She was the first of half-a-dozen pilot cutters to emerge from the yard, and the production line is continuing, although it takes a couple of years to complete a boat. In fact it takes much longer if you're a purist: piano concert technician (ie:

piano tuner to the stars) Malcolm McKeand has been working on *Kindly Light* for 14 years.

And then it'll be back to sea again the following day, provided the weather conditions allow.

In every sailing expedition there are moments of excitement when the gunwales disappear under water, the bowsprit buries itself into a wave, and the skipper has to shimmy up the mast. There are basking sharks to be spotted, and rescue missions to be run on yacht-loads of WAFIs – Wind Assisted F-ing Idiots – stuck on sandbanks.

But there is also plenty of time to learn how to sweat the throat, and what to do with the Lazy Jack. Sailing is a co-operative business – the tighter you can squeeze every squinch of sail, the closer you get to where you want to be – and it forges quick friendships. Expect to return unwashed, hairy-chinned (or whatever the feminine equivalent is) but happy.

Of course you don't have to be a bloke to do all this. *Eve* has plenty of women sailors, particularly on Women Go Wild weekends. They even had one who went ashore and returned an hour later to announce that she'd fallen pregnant. 'Cornish men don't work that fast,' explained the skipper. 'Apparently she'd been trying for a while and she'd thought she was just seasick, but she'd gone into town and bought herself a testing kit just to make sure.'

PRACTICALITIES

GETTING THERE

St Mawes sits on the opposite side of the water to Falmouth, on the end of the A3078. The nearest railway station (*www.nationalrail.co.uk*) is Falmouth, from where a foot ferry shuttles across to St Mawes.

TOURIST INFORMATION

Cornwall

❭ *01872 322900; www.visitcornwall.co.uk*

ACCOMMODATION

The Tresanton $ $ $ $

❭ *01326 270055; www.tresanton.com*

If you want to splash out without leaving the shore, St Mawes is home to one of Cornwall's boutique hotels.

BOATS

Classic Sailing

❭ *01872 580022; www.classic-sailing.co.uk*

From £280 for three nights on the *Eve of St Mawes*.

Further information about classic boat-building in Gweek can be found on *www.workingsail.co.uk*.

32

LINZ'S COBBLESTONE FIESTA

THE UNPRONOUNCEABLE PFLASTERSPEKTAKEL IN
LINZ ATTRACTS STREET PERFORMERS FROM ALL OVER
EUROPE, INCLUDING MANY FROM THE UK. THEY
CONVERGE ON THIS DANUBE CITY FOR THIS MAJOR
FREE EVENT. CREATIVE AND HILARIOUS.

A DANUBE CITY FAMOUS FOR ITS BRUCKNER FESTIVAL,
for Hermann Goering's mind-numbingly large
steelworks, and for being the birthplace of Adolf
Hitler doesn't exactly sound like a laugh a
minute. But there is a weekend in the year
when the streets of Linz fill with hundreds
of entertainers, jugglers and magicians,
many of them speaking English.

The city isn't a big tourism destination.
It isn't amongst the Alps and Mozart
wasn't born here, but it has a very well preserved nest of imperial
streets and squares which somehow escaped the steelworks-targeting
bombing raids of World War II, and it has deliberately set out to erase
those painful memories with a reputation as a happening place. The
highlight of its live and kickin' year is the Pflasterspektakel, a mecca
for street performers from all over Europe.

Actually, 'Pflasterspektakel' is a rotten name for an international
festival. Hard to spell, and even harder to say, it translates literally
as 'cobblestone entertainment', and you won't be surprised to learn
that it dates back to the Middle Ages when all sorts of traders would
gather in Linz's giant Hauptplatz, which was designed in the 13th
century to be the biggest square in Austria, being in a key location
on the river Danube.

Over the festival weekend in late July, it looks like that cornucopia
of races has returned: a very odd-looking collection of Belgians,

Estonians, Slovaks, Bohemians, Spanish, English *et al* ply an age-old trade around the Rococo central pillar – a trade that involves trying to please a cheering and booing mob in return for a few schillings.

In fact this festival is far more organised than in days gone by. Most of the performers are here by invitation of the committee, and a daily schedule is published distributing them around the 38 venues, most of which are in the pedestrian heart of the city. But there are no tickets sold and there is no obligation to remain as part of any audience for any longer than the performer can keep your attention. The only financial pain comes if you are still amongst that audience when the performance reaches its end and the hat comes round.

The variety is extraordinary. On a typical afternoon you might see a strange, Gothic-looking group from Belgium who enact an odd parable of the search for a suitable bride for their make-believe king, using stilts, drums and a wheeled metal chariot. Then there are two Hungarians dressed as bumblebees who run through a surreal selection of ballads, including *bara-bara-bara* (about 'the delight the shoemaker gets from smelling his leather').

Elsewhere there's an Indian magician doing rope tricks, a Slovakian jazz band, a *balalaika* band from Russia, bagpipers from Estonia and an Argentinian called Hugo who provokes howls of laughter when, after a seemingly accidental collision with an old lady making a determined beeline for a nearby church door, he reels away clutching a lacy black bra.

There will be quite a few Brits, and it is interesting to talk to them afterwards about the differences in attitude towards street performers in the UK and in mainland Europe. In Linz, they make good money from the crowd and are fêted as the latest exponents of an ancient tradition; in the UK, they're regarded as work-shy hippies who should get themselves a proper job. The British Arts Council is very reluctant to ever support a performer who works the street.

The Pflasterspektakel's biggest set piece takes place every evening at 22.00, when everything stops for a giant *samba* procession which moves slowly, rhythmically and hypnotically up through the square and out along the pedestrian streets, complete with real Brazilians in bikinis shaking their bits just like in Rio.

The procession will usually be followed by an extraordinary collection of strangely deformed caricature-creatures on stilts – a tiger, an elephant, a pig, a roast chicken, death, and a giant bird – stalking through the crowd and squabbling unintelligibly.

Linz does have a couple of other good reasons for visiting, if you can tear yourself away from the entertainment. Besides its position on the Danube, with boat tours to some of the best bits, there's a 537m hill in the city suburbs called the Postlingberg, ascended by a 110-year-old mountain railway, with original turn-of-the-century cars.

The mountain railway rises through orchards, stopping at little stations decorated with roses, and affording ever-widening glimpses of the city and the panorama beyond. At the top, the Postlingberg is crowned by a church and by the Grottenbahn, where punters ride the *Dragon Express* through an antique fairytale cave filled with gnomes in a variety of tableaux. It is so kitsch it's hard to keep a straight face.

Not a problem with the city's other big attraction, the Ars Electronica. Billed as Europe's only museum of the 21st century, it is housed in a compact glass building right on the Danube, and it focuses on state-of-the-art digital wizardry.

All the exhibits are interactive. Seek out the giant screen where you can use your own shadow to trap a deluge of letters and thereby make words. Try the virtual-reality tug of war, and also the small musical darting fish projected onto a velvet table top; you use a small selection of shapes to change its direction and thereby change its tune.

You never know, there might be something similar happening in the streets outside.

Linz's cobblestone fiesta

PRACTICALITIES

GETTING THERE

Ryanair (☎ *0871 246 0000; www.ryanair.com*) flies to Linz four times a week. Expect to pay from £120 return.

TOURIST INFORMATION

Austria

☎ *0845 101 1818; www.linz.at*

ACCOMMODATION

Hotel Wolfinger $ $ $

Right on the main square.

☎ *+43 732 773 2910; www.hotelwolfinger.at*

It can be tricky to find a room during the festival.

EVENTS/PLACES OF INTEREST

Pflasterspektakel

www.pflasterspektakel.at

Usually takes place in the last week of July.

Ars Electronica

☎ *+43 732 727 20; www.aec.at*

33

SLEEPING IN THE HAY IN NIEDERSACHSEN

THERE'S SOMETHING ROMANTIC ABOUT SLEEPING IN THE HAY, OR PERHAPS I AM CONFUSING MY THOMAS HARDY WITH 1970s' SOFT PORN WHERE FARM GIRLS CHOSE HAY BARNS FOR ENTHUSIASTIC RUMPY-PUMPY. EITHER WAY, SPENDING ONE'S DAYS IN THE SADDLE AND ONE'S NIGHTS IN THE HAY MAKES AN EXCELLENT OLD-FASHIONED ADVENTURE. PROVIDED YOU'RE NOT ALLERGIC.

NIEDERSACHSEN IS NOT ON EVERYONE'S TOURIST MAP; it's the largely flat, pastoral, German extension of the Netherlands, dominated by dairy farming and carved up by rivers and canals.

This landscape doesn't detain many passers-by, being too subtle to grab their attention from a speeding car and too widely spread for walking, but it does make ideal cycling country – big skies, no hills, not too hot, and cycle-only routes. It also has a unique network of 'hay hotels' where for a fixed price you get as much hay as you can sleep on, somewhere for a good hose-down, and a substantial nose-bag in the morning. Ee-aw!

One of the beauties of cycling is the creeping up on wildlife, through fields full of lapwings and bushes exploding with starlings. There'll be geese grazing in a distant meadow and curlews shrieking away over the floodplains, and the only other traffic will be the occasional postman's car, whose distant wheels approaching along the hardtop track will sound like someone sucking the last of a milkshake through a straw.

A couple of the more interesting cycle routes hereabouts converge on the Teufelsmoor – devil's moor – north of Bremen, where the

clouds knit together over the dykes in a disapproving frown and usually manage to amass a few devil's tears. Artists still gather in the creative community of Worpswede, to gaze intently at apple-cheeked farmers in baggy blue who are giving the shaggy flatlands a trim; for you, cycling through, every newly mown load could be a potential double bed.

Hay hotels (*Heuhotels* in German) are pretty egalitarian places; everyone gets the same level of comfort and there is, as yet, no posh top-of-the-range hay. Of the hay hotels around Worpswede, Farmer Reincke's is a former cattle stall in the front end of a typical brick-built Niedersachsen farmhouse. These huge buildings are half house, half barn, and many are hung with flower baskets and fronted by a display of retired farm machinery which the farmer has given a bright new coat of paint, as if to say 'you did me good service, and I'll see you right in your old age'.

The farmer is a cheery chap, and you might get a briefing on exactly what went wrong with his stock's artificial insemination this season, if your German is up to the technicalities. Moreover there's plenty of lore about the 'devil's moor' – stories of disappearing people, the cursing of cattle and the sheer infertility of the ground. All good stuff to be thinking about when it is just you, your sleeping bag, a couple of nesting birds, the hay, a good book, the dusk spilling through the open stall door, and a giant farm breakfast to look forward to.

Worpswede is itself an island, rising 52m above the boggy flats. It was its sense of grim isolation under moody skies which brought artists like Udo Peters and Maryan Zurek here at the turn of the

20th century for a sort of post-Impressionist, pre-Raphaelite Bloomsbury-in-the-bog.

Today the village is full of galleries, studios, smart hotels and restaurants with names like Artisst (literally 'art eats'). Two shire horses pull visitors around a selection of the 25-odd galleries, although visiting a couple of the big ones – the Worpswede Kunsthalle and the Grosse Kunstschau – is enough to get the general idea. More and more moor.

Worpswede's other local hay hotel, Mangels Breden, is tucked into rolling countryside on the northern side of the moor, up several miles of bumpy track. The dandelion-headed farmer's wife hums as she puts together cauliflower soup and cold meats for hungry cyclists, with a polythene bag to take away any leftovers in case you feel peckish in the night.

The barn is as big as an airport hangar, with an upstairs loft filled with giant rolls of hay and stables below to accommodate 17 horses, several cats and large quantities of chickens. Retire to your sleeping bag in the hayloft, when the bats begin to flicker in the roof space above, and like as not a patrol of farm cats will come marching through just as you've got down to your underwear. They'll stop to stare, and you can hear them saying to each other, 'Ist das der famous British beef?'

Unlike the majority of today's Germans, these farming communities in the north don't speak a lot of English, so some language ability will be handy if you want to get the best out of hay-hotelling. If you'd rather speak some English, then head for Karin Platte's farm at Langeloh, east of Worpswede, on the edge of fruit-growing country and with easy access from Hamburg. Frau Platte spent some time in the US, and she's combined Germanic thoroughness and American flair for marketing in turning her family farm into a charismatic place to stay, including the hay bit. A lovely woodland location, but don't expect to see much real farming going on, though.

PRACTICALITIES

GETTING THERE

EasyJet (↘ *0905 821 0905; www.easyjet.com*) has flights from Luton to Bremen for as little as £35 return. Worpswede is 15km northwest of Bremen.

TOURIST INFORMATION

↘ *020 7317 0908; www.germany-tourism.co.uk, www.niedersachsen-tourism.de* and *www.worpswede.de*

ACCOMMODATION

The region's hay hotels (Heuhotels) are marketed by Urlaub und Freizeit auf dem Lande (↘ *+49 42 319 6650; www.bauernhofferien.de*), where good English is spoken. The organisation will plan an itinerary depending on your time and arrival point and arrange for bicycle hire as well as reserve hay hotels in advance. All have dedicated showers and toilets, and a farm breakfast is included in the price. 🅢.

Farmer Reincke's hay hotel
↘ *+49 47 941 025; www.archehof-worpswede.de*
Mangels Breden
To the west by Osterholz-Scharmbeck
↘ *+49 47 952 60*
Karin Platte's farm
At Langeloh, near Tostedt, 50km southwest of Hamburg
↘ *+49 41 821 243; www.luetenshof.de*

34

GOING MULTI-MODAL IN THE WILDERNESS

PEDALLING OUT, PADDLING HOME, WEST SWEDEN. A REALLY UNUSUAL COMBINATION, THIS, INVOLVING HEADING OUT INTO A WATERY, MOOSE-INFESTED WILDERNESS ON A RAIL TROLLEY AND THEN RETURNING TO BASE BY CANADIAN CANOE. WITH THE OPTION OF A COUPLE OF NIGHTS OF CANOE-CAMPING ON ISLANDS *EN ROUTE*.

A *DRESSIN* IS A CYCLE-TROLLEY ORIGINALLY DESIGNED for railway workers setting out to do maintenance in the Swedish wilderness. It's not a beautiful beast: the cycle part is welded to a flat trolley for carrying tools, equipment and a passenger or two, albeit without the benefit of suspension. The whole thing is manoeuvrable by one person, but hernia-inducingly so, and you'd be doing well to get it to travel above 15mph on the level.

All in all these *dressins* are unwieldy things, but their advantage is the access they can give you to pretty wild country untouched by road. And those based in Dalsland in west Sweden give you just that, particularly once you've done the un-*dressin*, and changed from rail trolley to canoe. The result is the sort of experience which you'd normally expect in the remoter parts of Canada or Alaska.

In fact this Swedish journey does have an element of Atlantic-crossing, starting as it does at the Two Feathers Camp at Forsbackabaden, which comes complete with giant wigwam, axe-hurling range and larch-built ranch, all done in down-home cowboy movie style. In Sweden.

Two Feathers is the home of a jolly Swedish giant called John Brynteson, who also happens to be one-sixteenth Native American, and the rail/canoe combo is his creation, which he calls Daltrail. It starts on the disused railway to Svanskog, which runs by his back door, and returns via a network of lakes culminating in Lake Kalven, effectively his front door.

The rail trolley bit sets off into undulating forest, and on the downhill stretches you can get the wheels to go dum-diddle-ee, dum-diddle-aah. For about 10km you've got lakes on the right, and then another big one on the left, until you reach the tunnel that John will have warned you about. At this point you might have an attack of the heebie-jeebies, because tunnels are all very well in trains, but on rail-trolleys, without a torch, they're far more alarming. You've probably seen those Laurel and Hardy movies where the happy couple enter the tunnel on a platelayer's trolley, only to emerge seconds later pumping furiously, pursued by a locomotive... Well, the only trains on this route are occasional tourism charters (John knows the schedule) so you shouldn't worry. But you should still go 'wooo' all the way through, in case another *dressin* is coming the other way.

The hamlet of Svanskog, with supermarket and café, is the end of the line, at the end of an exhilarating downhill stretch. You're likely to be the only trolley at the platform, so you can make your own station announcements, viz: 'The train now leaving platform two is the 12.02 canoe express.' The un-*dressin* takes place at a place called Kroppan, about halfway back along the track, at a place where the railway crosses a narrow neck of water. John will have pointed this out in your pre-trip briefing, and he or a colleague will meet you here, at the edge of a forest trail, with the canoe.

At this point you have a choice, depending on available time, your prowess with a paddle and your taste for adventure. Out beyond your bows is a network of lakes connected by portage trails, where you put the canoe on a set of wheels to haul it a short distance between one lake and the next. In this way you could travel for weeks, from lake to lake, provided you have the right equipment.

Some of these lakes are free of human habitation, but with designated camping places on their shores. These camping places have fire pits which you might want to gather around in the evening, when the mosquitoes bite and the wolves howl. If you bed down here – John can provide the tent, stove, etc – you'll likely wake to a stunning scene of mist rising from the lake's surface and a moose browsing through the shore ferns.

Alternatively, if you're short of time, you can treat the whole experience as an exotic day trip, and paddle directly back from Kroppan through the 8km chain of lakes and narrows to the Two Feathers Camp at Forsbackabaden. Even this seems pretty remote, through a slowly changing vista of water, sky, diving birds, islands and trees. There will be wild animals amongst the birch and the pine, and blood-red wooden cabins on a couple of the islands, but you're unlikely to see anything or anyone during the main part of the day. The water, however, will be so clear that you can glimpse the tails of fish fleeing under your keel.

Even this route has a portage, so you will feel like you're on a real outback wilderness adventure, albeit a brief one. The portage gets you onto Lake Kalven, and eventually Daltrail's Two Feathers Camp will hove into view, complete with John's wigwam. If you've got any energy left, you can challenge the man himself to some axe-hurling, although I wouldn't back yourself to win.

PRACTICALITIES

GETTING THERE

Budget airline **Flyme** (✆ +46 770 790 790; *www.flyme.com*) operates between Stansted and Gothenburg, as also does **Ryanair** (✆ 0871 246 0000; *www.ryanair.com*). Expect to pay from £60 return.

From Gothenburg Central there's a two-hour train journey (timetables on *www.sj.se*) north to Dalsland, where John Brynteson will arrange pickup from his nearest station at Åmål on the Karlstad line.

TOURIST INFORMATION

✆ +46 318 183 00; *www.west-sweden.com*

ACCOMMODATION

By arrangement, either in a tent or Daltrail's big wigwam. $

ACTIVITIES

Daltrail

✆ +46 532 431 15; *www.daltrail.se*

The trolley-canoe combination from Forsbackabaden costs £50 for two people in peak season (12 June–27 August), and £40 the rest of the time. Additional canoe days cost £20; John can assist with camping equipment. The Daltrail website is *www.daltrail.se* (website currently Swedish only, but John will send out a brochure in English on request).

35

PILGRIMS AND *PULPERÍAS* IN GALICIA

THE GREEN CORNER OF NORTHWESTERN SPAIN IS
OFTEN OVERLOOKED, BUT ITS LANDSCAPE COMBINES
IRELAND WITH SWITZERLAND, IT HAS THE CHEAPEST
AND BEST SEAFOOD IN EUROPE, AND ONE OF
CATHOLICISM'S HOLIEST CITIES, SANTIAGO DE
COMPOSTELA.

THE RAIN IN SPAIN DOESN'T REALLY FALL UPON THE
plain at all; on the contrary, it favours the
country's rocky, steep northwestern corner,
where Iberia head-butts the Atlantic. Galicia, in
fact.

This is one of those places that looks
fabulous in photos, but photos don't tell
the whole story (as they don't with
Scotland and midges). Galicia has huge,
people-free golden-white beaches that

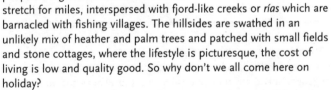

stretch for miles, interspersed with fjord-like creeks or *rías* which are
barnacled with fishing villages. The hillsides are swathed in an
unlikely mix of heather and palm trees and patched with small fields
and stone cottages, where the lifestyle is picturesque, the cost of
living is low and quality good. So why don't we all come here on
holiday?

Simple: Galicia gets 150 rainy days a year, and most holidaymakers
heading for Spain are seeking sun, not a soaking. Writer H V
Morton was so unimpressed that he dubbed Santiago de
Compostela a 'medieval aquarium'.

In fact the statistics are a touch misleading. Most of those
infamous days of rain are in the off-season, and the quantities of
grapes purpling on the local hill terraces testify to pretty healthy
levels of sunshine, too. But not as much sun, or as hot a sun, as

elsewhere in Spain; this is not a destination to pack just the itsy-bitsy bikini and the suntan oil, although you might need both.

There are plenty of other reasons to come. First, the sheer aesthetics of an Ireland-with-vineyards landscape, with that mixture of rock and sea, creek and beach, pasture and peasantry, and all of it swathed in a riot of greenery. It looks great, although you might not think so if you were a mariner caught in a storm off its Costa da Morte, the coast of death, west of A Coruña.

Then there's the seafood: ports of A Coruña, Vigo and Pontevedra are the home harbours of a significant proportion of the large Spanish fishing fleet, and I'm afraid to say that a lot of seafood caught by Scottish fishermen also ends up being trucked all the way down here too for onward distribution, so great is the demand. The result is that, instead of ubiquitous pizzerias, Galicia has *pulperías*, where octopus (*pulpo*) is the king of the menu. And it is cheap; a three-course fish-based menu won't cost you more than a dozen euros.

Then there's the culture. This is Europe's Celtic fringe, with echoes of Scotland, Ireland, and Brittany in its art and even in its language. Spend any time in local towns and villages and you'll like as not come across a bagpiper sooner or later.

And finally there's God, or more specifically His ambassador in the form of St James the Apostle ('Santiago' to the Spanish), whose bones are kept in the crypt of the cathedral in the city that bears his name, Santiago de Compostela. Those sacred bones are the focus of the biggest pilgrimage in Europe, our longest-lived example of mass tourism. The Camino, or pathway to the city, covers many hundreds of miles, and the ambitious walk all the way from the Pyrenees, seeking merit. During the summer, the squares around the cathedral are heaving with pilgrims, many of them clutching a staff and hobbling on blistered feet. Emergency oxygen is available for those who simply run out of steam.

Even for non-Catholics it is hard not to be gripped by the place and the catharsis of all that over-spilling faith, which is so dense that you can almost feel it brush your cheek.

The cathedral itself is a mixture of Romanesque and Baroque, and lavishly overdecorated on every square inch of its façade. Inside, it is filled with queues of pilgrims waiting to kiss the back of the saint's neck and touch foreheads with the building's architect.

The rest of the city centre – a UNESCO World Heritage Site – radiates outwards from the cathedral in a medieval nest of winding lanes and granite arcades, like a sort of lugubrious Rue de Rivoli. Every little square has a resident living statue, a puppeteer, a juggler or a musician, with bagpipes to the fore. And seafood restaurants galore, where happy pilgrims sit for happy hours, restoring their energy levels and making up for any deprivation suffered *en route*.

Once you've done Santiago and are intent on using that itsy-bitsy bikini, the best beaches are the Atlantic-facing sands at Vilar and Carnota, where the surf is pretty vigorous and the sand bleached white by the sun. Typical of the *ría* villages is Muros, crowded round a small port jammed with traditional boats and shoals of fish that no-one bothers to catch. There's a *pulpería* on the harbour front where you can fill up with the likes of fried squid, garlic chicken and spicy potatoes as well as octopus.

Of the three city-ports, Vigo, Pontevedra and A Coruña, the last is the most interesting, with tall, narrow lanes on a peninsula surrounded by water at every turn, and with a popular beach right in the city centre.

And then, finally, there's Finisterre, not to be confused with Brittany's Finistère, elsewhere in this book. Mind you, it is not just the name that's practically identical; this big bogey in Galicia's nose is also a big outcrop of rock with a desolate lighthouse once regarded as the end of the known world, just like in France. On calm days groups of hippies gather here to play their drums to the sea.

PRACTICALITIES

GETTING THERE

Ryanair (☎ *0871 246 0000; www.ryanair.com*). Expect to pay around £150 return.

TOURIST INFORMATION

www.turgalicia.es, www.santiagoturismo.com
Beach information (Vilar and Carnota) is on the *www.turgalicia.es* website under What to See, Natural Heritage.

CAR HIRE

Hertz
www.hertz.co.uk
Has cars at Santiago Airport from £29 a day.

ACCOMMODATION

Hotel Casa Rosalia S S
Os Anxeles, 10 miles west of Santiago
☎ *+34 981 887 580; www.hotelcasarosalia.com*
Good value, family-run hotel with pool and restaurant, between city and beach.

36

PICK YOUR OWN CHAMPAGNE

SPEND A MORNING HARVESTING THE GRAPES
YOURSELF AS A GUEST OF FAMILY-OWNED
CHAMPAGNE HOUSES IN L'AUBE, A BUCOLIC REGION
OF FRANCE NOT OFTEN VISITED BY TOURISTS. THE
HARVEST USUALLY TAKES PLACE IN LATE SEPTEMBER,
ALTHOUGH YOU CAN SET OFF ON A BACCHIC TOUR
ALONG THE CHAMPAGNE ROUTE AT ANY TIME OF
YEAR.

DESPITE ITS PRODUCT'S GLAMOROUS IMAGE AND OFTEN
extortionate cost, the main landscape that gives
us big-brand Champagne is a bit of a
disappointment. The industrial city of Reims
along with sedentary overgrown village
Epernay are at the heart of the industry,
with most of Champagne's big names,
but these are not exciting places and the
land around them is flat and uninspiring.
There's no hiding the fact that
Champagne is big business hereabouts.

AUBE EN
CHAMPAGNE

The industry gets more craftsman-like further south, however, in
the fizz-producing region of Aube en Champagne, south of the city
of Troyes. L'Aube ('the dawn of a promising morning') is an area of
reclining vineyards laced with clear, surging rivers and small,
geranium-splashed villages. And it is dotted with small, family-based
Champagne houses, including a handful which encourage you to
join in with the harvest in one of the few French wine regions where
the grapes are still picked by hand (which partly explains
Champagne's high cost). And if you have any kind of work ethic
then you'll understand that a good hard morning in the vineyard

makes a tipple or two a far greater pleasure in the afternoon. Moreover, this is a region where you can still buy a perfectly good bottle for half the UK price.

Troyes, as the gateway to this region, has a downtown area which is formed in the shape of a Champagne cork. That cork is filled with half-timbered houses which lean unsteadily towards each other, frozen in the act of whispered sweet-nothings. Many are grand city mansions built by former textile barons with mottos carved into the woodwork: 'Listen, consider, look – don't speak.' That message seems to include not making a big song and dance about Troyes's beauty, because despite being elegant and ancient, this is not a city even Francophiles know particularly well.

The countryside doesn't make big headlines, either. Gently rolling, pleasing on the eye, and studded with white-stoned hamlets like Les Riceys, considered to be amongst the most beautiful villages in France. Particularly notable is Essoyes, the village where Impressionist Pierre-Auguste Renoir spent most of his life in a modest house still lived in by descendants of the family. In Essoyes the river Ource, a tributary of the Seine, lingers long enough to admire the château, the half-timbered stables, the duck's bottoms and low-slung stone bridge, before surging onwards. Renoir found it 'as pure as villages can be', and it pretty much still is. His remains still rest here, in a tomb in the village graveyard.

Essoyes, Les Riceys and the sleepy town of Bar-sur-Aube are all on a meandering, 136-mile Champagne route through villages and hills which takes in the best scenery and threads together a variety of Champagne producers.

One of the most charismatic is the family Drappier, a medium-sized independent producer in the village of Urville. Drappier is presided over by the very welcoming and articulate Michel Drappier, who usually receives guests in person (and in English). He or his wife organise the annual *vendangeur* experience where visitors are kitted out with secateurs and spend the morning in the vineyards, doing as much, or as little, as they want. Then there's lunch with the pickers at noon, at long trestle tables set out in Drappier's loading depot. The professionals are mainly Poles (although Chinese are beginning to appear too) and the best of them can harvest 700kg – ten times their bodyweight – of grapes a day.

After lunch there's a guided tour of the production process, which is a good way to learn more about the Champagne story. About how, for example, Champagne really only came about by accident, midway through the 16th century. Relatively cool temperatures in these northerly vineyards meant that fermentation often wasn't complete before the end of the year, and it would restart when the weather warmed up again the following spring, by which time the wine was already in the bottle. The resulting effervescence became fashionable with the Parisian aristocracy.

These days Champagne production is an exact science and the producers are fiercely protective of the brand; even the 40-odd other towns and villages in France with 'Champagne' in their name are not allowed to put it on a bottle of anything. Go on the internet, however, and you might well find yourself a cheap case of Champing – made in Taiwan.

There are still some good deals to be found in L'Aube. I'd particularly recommend a small Champagne house in the very pretty village of Les Riceys called Champagne Guy de Forez. Here the Brut is light and delightful, and you'll get it for under £10. At that price it is worth slinging a box or two into the back of the car.

PRACTICALITIES

GETTING THERE

Cross the Channel with your own vehicle on any Dover–Calais route
(📞 0870 066 9612; *www.ferrysavers.co.uk*) – return prices from around £75.
Take the A26 past Paris, then the A5 towards Lyon, exiting at Troyes; a
journey time of around five hours.

TOURIST INFORMATION

The Aube en Champagne Tourist Board is based in Troyes (📞 +33 3 25 42 50
00; *www.aube-champagne.co.uk*). Pick up their Route du Champagne
brochure.

ACCOMMODATION

La Roseraie $ $
Essoyes
📞 +33 3 25 38 60 24; *www.laroseraie-en-champagne.com*
Very charming B&B accommodation in the heart of Renoir's home village.

CHAMPAGNE

Pick your own (usually at the end of September) is offered by **Champagne
Drappier**, in Urville (📞 +33 3 25 27 40 15; *www.champagne-drappier.com*), and
costs £30 person for a day including lunch and bottle of Champagne. A
handful of other Champagne houses in the Aube have a similar offer;
enquire at the tourist office in Troyes.

Champagne Guy de Forez is on Route de Tonnerre, Les Riceys (📞 +33 3 25 29
98 73).

HAMBURG'S ROCK 'N ROLL
FISHMARKET

37

EVERY SUNDAY STARTING FROM 05.00, LOCALS AND
VISITORS FLOCK DOWN THE FORMER FISH AUCTION
HOUSE ON THE QUAYSIDE BY THE ELBE TO DANCE,
DRINK AND BUY SMOKED EEL FROM SOME OF THE
RUDEST FISHMONGERS IN CHRISTENDOM. BIZARRE
BUT FUN.

THERE'S NOTHING LIKE ROCK 'N ROLL ON A SABBATH
dawn to jumpstart a flagging weekend. And
there's certainly nothing like rock 'n roll in the
Hamburg Fishmarket, complete with dawn buffet
of smoked eel and washed down with the first
Pilsener of the day. All consumed before
10.00 on a Sunday morn. A strange kind of
communion, indeed.

Hamburg is one of Germany's most
underrated city destinations, and the
closest in character to the UK. In fact, despite being twinned with
Shanghai, this is the most British of German cities, with an in-built
reserve that prevents it from making more of its attractions. Evidently
there's a tendency in the local character to hold oneself back that is
more British than the British themselves. This is, after all, the city
whose smart set wears pearls, cravates and corduroys, and whose
status car is a Jaguar, not a Mercedes-Benz. As the local saying goes,
'if it rains in London, the people of Hamburg put their umbrellas up'.

This city's traditional attractions are its lakes, its arts, its giant
port and its red-light district, the Reeperbahn. The Fishmarket is less
well known.

The Reeperbahn and the port grew together, with ships providing
most of the custom for the strip joints. These days, however,

container-ship quick-turnaround means that seamen/semen rarely get ashore, and the tourist board prefers the description 'former red-light district' for the Reeperbahn, placing the emphasis on all the musicals and cabarets along its length. Certainly you can come to see *Mamma Mia* here if you want, but there's a lot more on show than just Abba and discos, and most of it is not family fare.

The Fishmarket is more wholesome. It sits between the Reeperbahn and the water, set against a backdrop of dock cranes posing rhetorical questions against the sky. Its focal point is the fish auction hall, a multi-galleried, cantilevered, iron and glass cathedral, and on Sunday mornings it throbs with life.

Despite its name, fish play only a walk-on part in the proceedings. Amongst the stalls gathered around the hall it is the traders who are the big attraction, including the likes of Nudel Olli (speciality: stuffing bags with pasta), Banana Fred (speciality: hurling fruit) and Puten Peter (speciality: anything to do with chickens), all with big audiences and a patter which is heavily laced with salty humour. Some of them are celebrities, particularly Eely Dieter (speciality: hurling abuse) whose early-morning wit has earned him a lucrative TV career.

For those visitors not well versed in German innuendo the main attraction is inside the hall itself, where punters settle down at trestle tables that run the length of the nave, quaffing chilled litres. Above them, on the side galleries, caterers offer fish brunches with all you can eat for €15.

In here the rock 'n roll is in stereo, quite literally. At one end of the hall the lead singer of the Thunderbirds, in braces and beard and with the sweat pouring off him, preaches *Teenager in Love* to blurry up-all-nighters. And when he's run out of steam the lights go up at the other end, where disco band Miss Smith are waiting with *C'mon Baby Light My Fire*.

Then, almost on the stroke of 10.00, the ball is over. The tannoy speaks, the stalls close and the exhausted Cinderellas soak away into the side streets, clutching baskets of fruit and packets of greasy eels they never really wanted, with the whole of Sunday still stretched out before them.

If you are amongst those who have got up at dawn to drink, dance and be abused by an eel-monger, then you don't have to go far to find more entertainment.

Not far away is the Landungsbrücken, the clutch of pontoons for harbour tour boats, whose commentary is intended to make you round-eyed at the size of ships, the speed of container handling and the exotic list of destinations served. Definitely worth an hour of your time.

Beyond that starts the old warehouse city, the Speicherstadt, which now hosts an odd collection of attractions including Miniatur Wunderland, the world's largest model railway. In fact both name and billing don't do it justice. Miniatur Wunderland's micro landscapes of Hamburg, Germany and much of the rest of the world have been created with rare imagination and attention to detail; essentially, the trains are just an excuse for an extravaganza of storytelling, where the beauty is in the quirky detail. Blink and you'll miss the couple making love in the middle of a field of sunflowers. Blink again and you'll miss another couple making out in the Alps, this time being photographed by a voyeur while another man makes away with their underclothes. Etc.

And beyond the Speicherstadt lies a new development we'll all be hearing more about in the near future. HafenCity is a mixture of cultural, residential and corporate buildings which is a bit like London's Docklands, albeit in a more city-centre location. Its biggest single project is a concert hall called the Elbe Philharmonic, which is being built in the shape of a giant glass wave on top of a huge brick warehouse. The end result will be visually stunning, and it will do for Hamburg what Frank Gehry's Guggenheim Museum did for Bilbao.

And then there will certainly be more customers for early-morning rock 'n roll.

PRACTICALITIES

GETTING THERE

British Midland (☎ *0870 607 0555; www.flybmi.com*) has returns from Heathrow to Hamburg for around £150.

TOURIST INFORMATION

Hamburg
☎ *+49 40 300 513 00; www.hamburg-tourismus.de*
With a page devoted to the Fishmarket.

ACCOMMODATION

Galerie-hotel Sarah Petersen $ $
Lange Reihe
☎ *+49 40 249 826; www.galerie-hotel-sarah-petersen.de*
Unusual arty boutiquey guesthouse right by the railway station.

PLACES OF INTEREST

Miniatur Wunderland
☎ *+49 40 300 6800; www.miniatur-wunderland.de)*
Hafen City
www.hafencity.info

38

THE SOUK, THE CITADEL AND THE BARON OF ALEPPO

SYRIA'S SECOND CITY, ALEPPO, IS A MEDIEVAL SPICE-
TRADING CROSSROADS WITH A FABULOUS
LABYRINTHINE SOUK, LIKE SOMETHING OUT OF
INDIANA JONES. THIS IS A CULTURAL, HISTORICAL
AND ARCHAEOLOGICAL DESTINATION WHERE
FOREIGNERS ARE MADE WELCOME, DESPITE SYRIA'S
NEGATIVE WORLD IMAGE.

SYRIA IS FERTILE LAND FOR A TRAVELLER WHO ENJOYS culture shock. No matter what might be said about the nation's politics, its streets are very safe and its people are generally helpful and hospitable, as well as being blissfully free of the usual aspiration to wear jeans and eat hamburgers. In terms of flying time, it is not much further away than the likes of Cyprus or the Canary Islands; but in terms of culture, it might as well be a different planet.

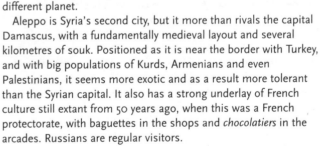

Aleppo is Syria's second city, but it more than rivals the capital Damascus, with a fundamentally medieval layout and several kilometres of souk. Positioned as it is near the border with Turkey, and with big populations of Kurds, Armenians and even Palestinians, it seems more exotic and as a result more tolerant than the Syrian capital. It also has a strong underlay of French culture still extant from 50 years ago, when this was a French protectorate, with baguettes in the shops and *chocolatiers* in the arcades. Russians are regular visitors.

The big reason for coming here at all is that covered souk, so intricately threaded under vaulted and domed ceilings that you need a ball of string – or a good nose for spiced air – to find your way out. In essence, it feels like a collection of long inter-connected cathedral naves, each with its own specialist merchants, with side-openings at intervals into cloistered caravanserai. These are huge courtyards with accommodation for visiting merchants upstairs and trading space below. In other circumstances they might make glorious hotels – a couple of small palaces elsewhere have been beautifully converted – or at the very least be piled high with myrrh and frankincense. Not bales of flip-flops, as they are today.

Make your way through all this to the far end of the souk, taking care not to collide with heavily laden donkeys, and you will emerge eventually at the foot of the citadel. The citadel is a monstrous 12th-century fortress knuckled with battlements and towers, and with an entrance corridor that twists and turns to give the defenders every chance of beating off the invading hordes. There are also great views from the top.

Commercial, downtown Aleppo is made up of boulevards of six-storeyed apartments that could have been airlifted from Hausmann's Paris, and key amongst them is Abu Riesheh Street, the city's Champs-Elysées, lined with fountains and big-windowed cafeterias. Here well-heeled businessmen drink beer, smoke hubble-bubble and eat homemade pistachio ice cream, while hawkers outside sell anti-impotence oil to teenagers who don't want to be found wanting when the big day comes.

You won't get much of a public display of affection in this society, but lovers sit side by side on the benches in the city's central park. The park was modelled on the Parisian Jardins de Luxembourg, with tree-lined gravel walkways, statues of poets and knee-high clipped hedges. The only thing missing is a game of *boules*.

Elsewhere in the city it is worth searching out the Baron Hotel, one of the Middle East's classic addresses. Largely un-reconstructed, its fixtures and fittings belong to a 1930s' prep school common room, and its staff number several old retainers who've worked there for more than 30 years. Previous guests include the likes of Agatha Christie and Lawrence of Arabia, and it remains in the ownership of the Armenian family who built it. Most of the hotel's original clients will have arrived at Aleppo via the railway station, in grand period trains like the *Taurus Express*, direct from Istanbul. The station itself is a strange orientalist construction with painted ceilings and marble floors, and the setting for the opening scene in Agatha Christie's *Murder on the Orient Express*.

Aleppo is surrounded by ancient history, and many agencies in the town offer trips out to the so-called 'Dead Cities', late Roman and early Byzantine ruins strewn across the north of the country. Here 1,500-year-old monasteries, temples and churches still stand in landscapes which have proved too arid for modern settlement, which is why the stones have never been borrowed to make newer houses.

The big destination amongst the 700-odd Dead Cities is the complex at Deir as Sama'an, which was originally built around the hill called Jebel Sama'an to cope with the overflow of pilgrims attracted by eccentric ascetic, Simeon Stylites. It was on Jebel Sama'an that Stylites chained himself to the top of a pillar, eventually becoming a medieval tourist attraction.

Simeon was born in AD390 to a shepherd's family, but at the age of 16 he was already wearing a spiked girdle and spending his summers buried up to his chin in the ground. Word of his ferocious asceticism spread and gained him quite a fan club – so he climbed up his 64ft pillar to escape the crowds, never to come down again.

A huge basilica was built around his pillar after his death. Today it is a well-preserved ruin with a commanding view over rolling plateaux, patched with olive and pistachio fields all the way towards the Turkish border. The pillar itself, framed by delicate arches, has been reduced to a sad, shapeless rock by centuries of souvenir hunters. Amazingly, Simeon remained rooted to it for a full 30 years, which rather beats anything by David Blaine.

PRACTICALITIES

GETTING THERE

British Midland
☎ *0870 6070 555; www.flybmi.com*
Direct flights for around £340 return.

TOURIST INFORMATION

www.syriatourism.org

ACCOMMODATION

Beit Wakil $ $
Aleppo
☎ *+963 21 211 7083; www.beitwakil.com*
Stylish conversion of former merchants' palace-cum-caravanserai.
Baron Hotel
☎ *+963 21 210 880*
On Baron Street, in the newer part of town.

PLACES OF INTEREST

All hotels and on-street travel agencies will be keen to take you to the Dead Cities/Deir as Sama'an. Prices negotiable, but not more than £50 for the day.

AUTUMN

Summer may be over, but that's no reason for staying home. The sea hasn't yet cooled as much as the land, which is why I recommend a quick dash to Pembrokeshire to try coasteering before it gets too wild. You can get wet, too, on Scotland's Rannoch Moor, but that'll be the rain coming in sideways; never mind, there's a great sleeper train journey to get you here and back again. Of course, you don't necessarily have to travel to experience culture shock; there's plenty of that in London's Docklands and East End. And if all of that seems completely mad, then you might be ready for a spiritual retreat in a monastery in Leicestershire which has guest accommodation. (*HOME FRONT* 39–42)

Across the water, autumn is a great time to be visiting Ireland's southwestern extremities, the last bony peninsulas of County Cork. It's also a good moment to head for the French Riviera, and tease out all the surprisingly Russian connections of a place that's meant to be moderately British: Nice. For a bit of continental indulgence without damaging the ozone layer there's always the Belgian city of Ghent, a more businesslike Bruges. And if you've got an open mind on what constitutes tourism then try Germany's Ruhr Valley, which is to be European Capital of Culture in 2010, and see what a pretty coal mine really looks like.

To wrap up the year, I'm suggesting a way of going on wintry cruises but without going far or paying through the nose by using long-distance ferries; a pre-Christmas shopping trip to the world's oldest republic, San Marino; and a weekend visit to one of Germany's loveliest and most ancient Christmas markets in a city with a very colourful recent past, Nuremberg. (*MEDIUM DISTANT* 43–50)

The last two weekends in this book have little in common. For a taste of iridescent leaf-fall with some terrifically energetic music-making, I'm recommending Canada's Cape Breton for the Celtic Colours Festival in early October. And for something of Nepal but without the jet lag, I'm suggesting a weekend in Morocco's Atlas Mountains, based at a kasbah run by a Bedouin–British partnership. Very ecologically sound. (*FURTHER FLUNG* 51–52)

PRICE GRADING FOR ACCOMMODATION

$ – up to £40 for a double room; $$ – £40–70 double;
$$$ – £70–110 double; $$$$ – £110 + double.

DESTINATIONS

HOME FRONT

MEDIUM DISTANT

FURTHER FLUNG

WETSUITS AND WINTER SWELLS IN WALES

39

A COCKTAIL PARTY WITH A DIFFERENCE, WITH A DRESS CODE OF NEOPRENE AND RUBBER. THE INTOXICATION COMES FROM A SERIES OF NATURAL HIGHS FROM A MENU OF ADRENALIN COCKTAILS, AND TOP AMONGST THEM IS COASTEERING, WHICH WILL HAVE YOU BOBBLING AROUND IN THE SURF, BUMPING INTO THE CLIFFS, AND GIGGLING.

WHOEVER CAME UP WITH THE IDEA OF WRAPPING UP willing souls in wetsuits and then trolling them along the foot of sea cliffs could never have dreamed how it was going to catch on. Come rain or shine, there's bound to be a group of initiates bobbling around off the British coastline somewhere or other, and having a surprisingly good time.

Kite-surfing may have grabbed the headlines in recent years, but it is fiendishly hard to the point of being well nigh impossible, and it takes an age just to master the gear. Coasteering is far more accessible for ordinary mortals, and you don't need to practise to make it perfect.

WALES COAST

At first sight it doesn't seem fun at all. In fact, coasteering is the closest a human being could ever get to understanding what a pair of underpants has to undergo each time they go into the washing machine. Sloshed and bludgeoned in suds and froth, catching momentary glimpses of the world as it revolves, with trousers wallowing by and the occasional wandering sock in your face. Followed by spin, barnacle scrub and Atlantic rinse.

Except this isn't the laundrette, the surf doesn't come in a box, and the sock has a foot in that belongs to another nutcase like you, all of you a couple of smiles away from the asylum.

The art of coasteering was actually first mentioned in an early 20th-century guidebook to north Devon. The idea is to do a traverse along the land/sea interface, through the only bit of our environment that we human beings have yet to devise a vehicle for. You don't need equipment, or lessons, to do this, and a combination of wetsuits and adrenalin is sufficient protection from the cold. Moreover you're unlikely to get lost, given that the sea is on one side on the way out, and the other on the way back.

The spiritual home of coasteering is Pembrokeshire, adventure sport paradise, and walkers on the coast path are getting used to seeing brightly coloured bodies being sloshed around where the surf meets the rock. They no longer call out the emergency services, but that doesn't mean they understand what's going on; could it be fish farming with attitude? Hydroponic skateboarding? Extreme orienteering?

One of the experienced providers of adventure sports hereabouts, Preseli Venture, offers coasteering within a menu of endorphin-blasting Adrenalin Cocktails, along with sea-kayaking and hiking. Autumn is a particularly good time, because the sea has just passed its peak warmth (September) and the winter swells are beginning to make the process more interesting.

That may make it sound dangerous, but Preseli say they get more bumps and scrapes from the mountain biking. Perhaps the most gruelling bit is clambering into a cold wetsuit in the equipment shed beforehand ('we like to keep them moist for you,' joke the guides). In full gear, you'll feel a bit like the man from Milk Tray looking for a novel way of delivering a box of chocolates.

Coasteering ends with optional jumping. This is a sort of watery bungy jump but without the bungy, and involves hurling yourself off a cliff into deep water. It sounds horrendous, but if you start off at a low level, your confidence grows fast. And it certainly helps if you swear like buggery on the way down.

As for the mind-altering, endorphin-blasting effects of the sport, it depends on who you ask. Preseli's view is that outdoor activities alter the physiological state more than any other substances, and that by the end of the day clients will be on a major endorphin high.

The only Es involved in all this euphoria are of the 'wheeeee' variety. Mind you, Preseli's bar does offer legitimate herbal additives in the form of its so-called Brain Boosters (containing gingko biloba to boost the brain's energy), Ginseng Hammers (with ginseng and kava kava to enhance energy) and Relax Juice, with hops and lavender to produce a relaxed yet alert state of mind. And if none of the above does the job, then there is always the Hobgoblin ale.

Certainly sea-swimmers in general enthuse about the mind- and body-enhancing benefits of bathing in the mastery of the forces of nature. They believe that the act is physically and spiritually uplifting, a natural antidepressant, and can even heighten perception. After all, it was only a decade ago that Margate had the Royal Sea Bathing Hospital, based on the curative properties of cold-water immersion.

On its residential Adrenalin Cocktail weekends Preseli tends to host a lot of overseas students on attachments in the UK, mostly from America. The upside of having US high school kids around is that many of them are reassuringly unathletic (ie: fat), indicating that this activity is not just the preserve of hard men with bunched thighs, wraparound shades and an affected Aussie twang. The downside is finding oneself permanently in conversations about how Texans are crud and people from Ohio are nice.

But they do express themselves interestingly in the comments book. 'Coasteering ripped,' writes one. 'The H_2O took my breath away,' writes another. 'I'm a boat,' says a third. And a fourth chips in with the rather surreal 'ride the horses! milk the cows!'

PRACTICALITIES

GETTING THERE

By train (*www.nationalrail.co.uk*) to Haverfordwest, from where Preseli Venture will pick up pre-booked passengers.

TOURIST INFORMATION

Pembrokeshire

☏ *01437 763110; www.visitpembrokeshire.com*

ACCOMMODATION

Preseli Venture $ $ $

☏ *01348 837709; www.preseliventure.co.uk*

Provides all board, lodging and equipment at its home base near the village of Mathry. The lodge has a bar, wood-burning stoves and accommodation for up to 30 people. All inclusive.

40

THE 21.15 TO RANNOCH MOOR

TAKE THE SMOG-TO-BOG SLEEPER TRAIN TO BRITAIN'S
GREATEST WILDERNESS. FALL ASLEEP IN THE SUBURBS
OF LONDON AND WAKE UP ON SCOTLAND'S RANNOCH
MOOR, WHERE THERE'S A SURPRISING CHOICE OF
STATIONS RIGHT IN THE MIDDLE OF NOWHERE. EACH
HAS SOMEWHERE DISTINCTIVE TO STAY.

FOR PEOPLE WHO APPRECIATE THE POWER AND THE
glory of wild country there's nothing quite like
Rannoch Moor. No roads dare to cross this 56
square-mile welter of bog and rock and you'd be a
fool to try to cross it on foot without making
elaborate preparations beforehand.

Mankind has, however, added his stitch to the fabric
in the shape of the London to Fort William railway line,
which weaves right across the middle. In places the
ground is so boggy that the track has had to be laid
on a floating raft of logs. Trains are infrequent and
puny amongst all this immensity, but there is one
special procession of coaches that rattles over the
moor every day, ironing the floating track flat: the Caledonian sleeper,
which runs between London Euston and Fort William. This overnight
train acts as a kind of Tardis: you step in amongst London's crowds
and black cabs, fall asleep to the rhythm of passing points, and step
out amongst Rannoch's deer and midges.

Amazingly, there's a choice of two stations on the moor. One is
Corrour, where there are no roads at all, and the other Rannoch, at
the road-head of a thin tarmac strip which struggles all the way
across from the A9 at Dalwhinnie.

Corrour, whose station was originally built to service a big deer-
hunting lodge that burned down, is the tougher posting of the two.

The former bunkhouse in the old signal box parked on the station platform is sadly no longer in use. Instead, there's bed and breakfast in the relatively new Station House, or the option of staying in one of Britain's most remote youth hostels, on the shores of Loch Ossian a mile away. The hostel, which has a history of eccentric hostel-keepers, is solar- and wind-powered and even painted in bat-friendly paint, but it closes to passing trade in the winter months, during which time it can be rented as a complete building (20 beds). If you are on the sleeper and you want to get off at Corrour, you'll need to tell the train guard well in advance, because this is a request stop.

There's considerably more comfort at Rannoch, with a proper hotel in the shape of the Moor of Rannoch, albeit with just five bedrooms. The hotel was originally built as a necessary sanctuary for railway workers, and it has developed its own distinctive style. The bar sells beers brewed by monks and Orkney fishermen; gables of driftwood surround the bookcases; bathrooms are wood-panelled like Swiss chalets, and a couple of the guest beds are mounted on weather-beaten thrones made out of old deer fences and snow barriers from the moor. Expect open fires all year round, a venison stew slow-cooking on the Aga and a fabulous view from every window.

Meals are served downstairs in the conservatory, also with views in mind, although gruesome local weather conditions can sometimes prevent you seeing anything at all. High points of the day are the arrival of the post-bus, often with essential hotel supplies, and the departure of the trains. There's no TV, and mobile phones don't work – which is exactly why people come here.

It is certainly why current proprietors Rob and Liz Conway gave up their careers in England. Over the years the Conways had come regularly to stay in the hotel, and when they heard the owners were moving on – after trying to home-school their son in a camper van outside the hotel – they simply couldn't ignore the opportunity. 'I never wanted to be in the hotel trade; I just wanted to live here,' says Rob.

Apart from feasting on venison and grazing through the library there's not a lot in the way of formal entertainment, so all the guests talk to each other, creating an informal house party. A multi-national one, too. You could easily find yourself sharing a table with Parisians, or Dutch, or New Zealanders. Americans regularly turn up, full of anxious talk about what might happen if they step outside and twist their ankle or lose the path.

And then there's all that fresh air. There's good river and loch fishing in season, particularly in the sandy-shored Loch Laidon where the ripples over shallow rocks look like otters playing. You can also walk forever, particularly on the Road to the Isles, a former drover's track which keeps to high (and dry) ground, and goes all the way to Ullapool. On a long weekend, though, you should restrict yourself to trudging along the track as far as Corrour, where you can wait for the next train back.

Whether you choose to base yourself in more primitive conditions at Corrour or in more luxury at Rannoch, be sure to climb up one of the local hills and look back. From a distance, the lochs appear to be bits of sky fallen to ground. The occasional train, moreover, looks like a metal caterpillar crawling across the moor's face to deliver another nutcase or two to this strange kind of sanctuary.

Think of it as a kind of Priory for those who believe in purification by isolation.

The 21.15 to Rannoch Moor

PRACTICALITIES

GETTING THERE

Caledonian sleepers, run by **Scotrail/First Group**, leave London Euston every night except Saturday; ditto from Rannoch/Corrour (☎ *0845 601 5929; www.firstgroup.com/scotrail*). A return with a berth will cost from £120.

TOURIST INFORMATION

Fort William
☎ *08452 255121; www.visithighlands.com, www.corrour.co.uk*

ACCOMMODATION

Moor of Rannoch Hotel $ $ $
Rannoch Station
☎ *01882 633238; www.moorofrannoch.co.uk*
The Station House $
Corrour
☎ *01397 732236*
Offers B&B.
Loch Ossian Hostel
A mile from Corrour
☎ *0870 155 3255; www.syha.org.uk*
The Scottish Youth Hostels Association maintain this hostel.

41

CONCRETE AND CULTURE SHOCK IN THE EAST END

YOU DON'T HAVE TO BASH A HOLE IN THE OZONE LAYER TO EXPERIENCE CULTURE SHOCK. THERE'S A HEADY DOSE OF ASIA MUCH CLOSER TO HOME, AROUND LONDON'S BRICK LANE, AND IT IS WITHIN SHOUTING DISTANCE OF OUR MOST BRASH MINI CHICAGO, DOCKLANDS. COMBINE THE TWO FOR A TOTAL CHALK-AND-CHEESE WEEKEND.

THE DOCKLANDS LIGHT RAILWAY IS A DIBBLY-DOBBLY affair. It departs from the City pretending to be a serious train, but once it gets to Docklands it swerves and dives through imaginary hills and valleys, braking suddenly for no apparent reason and then surging on again. Alone, you might be tempted to sit in the front window (DLR is computer-controlled, so there's no driver's cabin) and make driver-type noises, but you're likely to be surrounded by captains of industry looking dignified and important, so I wouldn't, if I were you.

LONDON'S EAST END

Get off at Canary Wharf. If it's a weekday, you'll feel an instant cultural alienation amongst all the pinstripes and stilettos. There's a swagger in the air here, because if you're in a suit and working in Canary Wharf, you're in your prime, and destined for great things.

If it's a weekend the place will be pretty quiet, but you can still admire the forest of giant towers, the curved glass, the big shiny steel columns and the moving neon writing that speaks a Dow–Nikkei language only the natives understand. This is big money expressing itself in a way that it hasn't been able to do anywhere else in London, and if you're very sensitive, you might be able to detect motion under your feet: the place is riddled with

fitness centres. Where once workers burrowed underground to find coal, now high achievers go down there to get sweaty.

There are only a couple of boats still in these docks, and one is a floating church – St Peter's Barge – for when it all gets too much. It's parked at Heron Quay outside one of the few original warehouse buildings, now housing the Museum in Docklands, where you can go if you want to see what all of this once looked like. Not so long ago.

Back on the dibbly-dobbly DLR, head further east beyond the Brave New World, and you emerge into industrial wasteland near City Airport. Get off at Pontoon Dock on the George V branch and step into Thames Barrier Park, a Modernist public garden with a glassed pavilion and hedge designs that echo the shapes of the barrier itself. The barrier looks disappointingly puny these days, or is it just that we now know that global warming has effectively posted a 'sell by' date on its shell? It won't be able to protect London from rising seas. Across the water from Pontoon Dock is the sleek shape of a cruise liner, actually the Sunborn Yacht Hotel, one of the accommodation suggestions for this weekend (see *Practicalities* below).

Having seen something of Docklands, return on the DLR, change to the Tube and emerge at Aldgate East. The contrast will hit you between the eyes; scruffy, ancient, urban, multi-cultural East End. It's also dead trendy and arty, and the Whitechapel Art Gallery is right here by the Tube station, one of London's cutting-edge exhibition venues. Enter, and you may well find yourself watching a film of people debating the meaning of a particular Croatian folk song. Interesting.

Turn left just up beyond Aldgate East and you'll be headed up to Brick Lane, past sari shops, spice traders, leather-jacket makers and even an estate agent selling property in Dubai, indicating that the setting for Monica Ali's bestseller *Brick Lane* is not all about Third-World living; there's money here too.

The air smells of curry and rings with the sounds of Bollywood. There are women in yashmaks, Bangladeshi elders with goatee beards and shops piled high with jackfruit and sugarcane. Bright neon boutique restaurants with names like Chutneys, Saffron and Poppadum will have smooth-talkers out front, murmuring about discounts and free bottles of wine as you pass. If you ever wanted to eat a bargain chicken tikka under a giant mural of Princess Diana, then you'll find it here.

But Brick Lane isn't just about Bangladeshis and chapatis. Further north, up by the Truman Brewery, it acquires a very hip, urban vibe with uber-trendy boutiques and vintage clothes emporia. The curry houses are replaced by fashionable caffs where art students hang out with their laptops and their French cigarettes. On Sunday mornings this stretch transforms itself into a street market for the locals, and has a far more eclectic collection of traders than at neighbouring Petticoat Lane, where all the tourists go. Lots of Brick Lane stuff will have fallen off the back of a lorry and be sold by people who haven't heard of eBay.

Up at the top end of Brick Lane there are two 24-hour hot bagel (here spelled 'beigal') shops much loved by Jewish taxi drivers and true East Enders. And if you turn right at the top into Bethnal Green Road you'll come eventually to Kelly's pie 'n mash shop, which is straight out of the *EastEnders* hymnal: bare tiled walls, marble tables, strip lighting and a tough-talking old dear called Iris, who deposits the mash on your plate with a thud.

If you've experienced all of this and still have room for more, then branch west from Brick Lane across to Spitalfields Market, the East End's version of Covent Garden. The permanent shops are pretty eclectic (look out for the outrageously kitsch boutique called Queens), but the stalls inside haven't quite made up their mind whether to be cheap or chic.

From here it's a short walk back to Aldgate East.

PRACTICALITIES

GETTING THERE

Take the Docklands Light Railway eastwards from Bank or Tower Hill. Or the District Line to Aldgate East.

TOURIST INFORMATION

www.visitlondon.com

ACCOMMODATION

City Hotel `$ $`–`$ $ $`
Osborn Street (Brick Lane)
☎ *020 7247 3313; www.cityhotellondon.co.uk*
Phone for deals.
Sunborn Yacht Hotel `$ $ $ $`
Close to City Airport
☎ *020 7059 9100; www.sunbornhotels.com*

PLACES OF INTEREST

Thames Barrier Park
www.thamesbarrierpark.org.uk
Docklands Museum
☎ *0870 444 3857; www.museumindocklands.org.uk*
St Peter's Barge
☎ *020 7093 1212; www.stpetersbarge.org*
Whitechapel Art Gallery
☎ *020 7522 7888; www.whitechapel.org*
Brick Lane Market
www.eastlondonmarkets.com
Spitalfields Market
www.visitspitalfields.com

THE CISTERCIANS OF CHARNWOOD FOREST

42

IT'S BEEN A HARD YEAR, AND YOU DESPERATELY NEED
A BREAK, BUT ONE THAT WILL REFRESH YOUR MIND
AND SPIRIT AS WELL AS YOUR BODY. SO RETREAT TO
MOUNT ST BERNARD ABBEY, NEAR LEICESTER, WHERE
ACCOMMODATION HAS NO COST – ALTHOUGH YOU
CAN MAKE A CONTRIBUTION. YOU DON'T HAVE TO BE
RELIGIOUS, BUT IT HELPS.

A RETREAT IS A CONCEPT WHICH IS YOURS FOR THE
making. For some it is a spiritual experience to
be shared with like-minded companions; for
others it is a period of self-imposed solitary
confinement, a chance to wrestle with your own
demons, or simply to leave the little demons at
home to do the washing up for once. Whether or not
your retreat has a religious component is largely a
matter of personal choice – and the choice of your
host institution, whichever, whatever or wherever
that may be.

**MONASTIC
RETREAT**

There's no doubting the spiritual credentials of
Mount St Bernard Abbey, near Leicester. This is
one of the most austere Christian communities in the country, and
its 35 Cistercian monks lead lives dedicated to prayer and penitence,
mostly in silence.

But the monastery guesthouse is a different matter; here there's no
requirement for prayer or penitence, but don't come here expecting
cocktails and karaoke either. People who come on retreats tend to do
so for very good reasons. If you are not at ease in the presence of piety,
then you might find group meal times an uncomfortable experience.

When the Cistercians first arrived at Mount St Bernard from France
back in 1835, the land they bought was as unforgiving as their daily

lives. The Charnwood Forest may not be particularly high or wild, but these raw, bony hills attract the snow when neighbouring areas of Leicestershire do not, and it took a great deal of back-breaking labour to prepare for the planting of gardens, orchards and corn fields.

The unstinting effort of this pioneering handful of monks deeply impressed the local aristocracy, who clubbed together to fund a proper monastery building designed by Augustus Pugin, architect of the Houses of Parliament; he gave his services for free. The result is an impressive, powerful-looking knuckle of stone – farm, walled garden, abbey church, cloister and guesthouse accommodation – set in sloping lawns amongst hedgehog hills, whose trees bristle like scrubbing brushes in the bleaker months of the year. There's a real sense of peace up here, broken occasionally by the bark of a farm dog rising up from below, and the distant lowing of penned-in cattle dreaming of skylarks and grass.

When it opened, Mount St Bernard was the first monastery to be built in Britain after the Reformation. Sightseers visited in their hundreds, and in the early years celebrated politicians and literary figures – William Wordsworth and Florence Nightingale, for example – came here on retreat, seeking inspiration from the spirituality of the community.

Today the Cistercian order is not as rigorously ascetic as it used to be. Until the 1960s there was an obligation to silence, the community ate no fish or meat, slept on straw mattresses in dormitory cubicles, and conducted services in Latin in the abbey church, invisible from the public gaze. These days the church is open-plan, although for the majority of the seven daily services the only voices are those of the monks, communicating with their God. Today they have their own rooms and their diet is far more varied, although still vegetarian. Their day still starts at 03.15, and they still have no live TV, no newspaper or radio except by special permission, with an obligation to silence for six hours a day. They also make a will disposing of all their possessions before they enter the monastery.

What certainly hasn't changed is their appetite for work, be it academic, spiritual, physical or domestic. The monks do their own cleaning and cooking, farming and clothes-making, and try to do as much of the maintenance and repair work on the property as they can. But their numbers are dwindling – currently at around half the level of 50 years ago – and they're not being replaced. There was a time when monasteries like this would take novices direct from school, but these days postulants have to have had some sort of outside life first, and many don't make it all the way through to final vows, a process which can take at least two years.

And so the hardcore goes on getting older. Nearly all are over 60 and Father Peter is in his mid seventies, but that doesn't stop him from planting the potato crop by hand. Most durable of them all is Father Theodore, who for the last 35 years, summer and winter, has been leading the life of a hermit in a former duck shed in a copse in the middle of a nearby field. There he continues to strictly observe the monastic timetable of services, in Latin, complete with the habitual 03.15 start. His solitude – but not his vow of silence – is broken once a day when he returns to the monastery to collect the ingredients for his meals.

Despite their advancing ages, the St Bernard monks continue to support themselves. Much of their daily bread comes from their own gardens. Their farm sells milk to the trade, they have a shop with a stock of books, homemade candles and religious artefacts, and the St Bernard pottery sells as quickly as it is made.

And although they have taken strict vows of chastity, they do have their admirers. Most of the shop's clientele comprises ladies of a certain age, many of whom are regular visitors. Most of the monks are nonplussed by this attention, but these admirers, combined with legacies from benefactors and donations from guesthouse visitors like you, help keep the whole place afloat.

PRACTICALITIES

GETTING THERE

The abbey is just off the M1, 12 miles northwest of Leicester, near the town of Coalville.

TOURIST INFORMATION

Leicester
☎ 0906 294 1113; www.goleicestershire.com

ACCOMMODATION

Mount St Bernard Abbey ⑤
Coalville
Guestmaster (☎ 01530 839162; www.mountsaintbernard.org)
Funded by donations.

CORK'S BONY FINGERS

43

A COUNTRY HOUSE WEEKEND IN COUNTY CORK,
WHERE IRELAND'S FINEST PENINSULAS WAGGLE THEIR
BONY FINGERS IN THE SEA. DRAMATIC SCENERY,
GOOD FOOD AND GREAT CHARACTERS POPULATE A
COASTAL REGION NOT QUITE AS FAMOUS AS THE
NEIGHBOURING RING OF KERRY, BUT ALL THE
BETTER FOR BEING SO.

A LOT OF WEALTHY EUROPEANS HAVE BOUGHT
property in Ireland's County Cork these days,
and you can see why. The landscape –
rugged coastal peninsulas backed by lush
river-fed fields – is one reason why people like
Jeremy Irons and David Puttnam have
chosen to live here, many of them in
grand houses or castles that were once at
the centre of feudal estates. This influx of
wealth has brought employment to a
struggling area and raised the standards of food and
accommodation.

For this weekend the focus is on two of the peninsulas and clear-
water bays of west Cork, described by poet Seamus Heaney as
'water and ground in their extremity'. Mizen Head and Sheep's
Head frame inlets with cormorants, seals, and mussel farms. This is
a place to make discoveries, meet eccentrics and maybe even
develop a few eccentricities yourself.

The Cork coastline has been a hard taskmaster and local
emigration has been dramatic. Famine laid waste to whole villages
and the map is thick with *cillín* (famine burial grounds), but tourism
has led a mini-revival and multi-coloured paintpots have
transformed many a high street. Surprisingly, the endemic

communities of small farmers and fishermen don't seem to resent the incoming settlers at all; in fact the natives and the newcomers derive much mutual amusement from each other's perceived eccentricities.

Mizen Head is the more cosmopolitan and sophisticated of the two peninsulas, with the appealing village of Schull as the key centre. Schull is west Cork's equivalent of Salcombe, with a strong yachtie flavour. Over the years a selection of arts-and-crafts shops, delicatessens, cafés and restaurants have found their niche on the village's short main street. So much so that Schull has been dubbed 'the food capital of Ireland' by the respected food writers Sally and John McKenna – who happen to live locally. Look out for striking German silversmith Sabine Lenz in her shop Enibas, and don't overlook Annie's Restaurant a bit further north in Ballydehob, a tiny venue which earns deep respect for its unswervingly traditional menu of the likes of garlic mussels and roast rack of lamb. A real institution is the pre-dinner drink across the road in Levi's, a pub-cum-grocery store run by two old ladies, who like to have a good long look at Annie's dinner guests before Annie gets them herself.

Mizen Head's scenery gets better the further south you go, with several fine beaches and views out to the Fastnet Rock (as in the shipping forecast). The Mizen Head Visitor Centre has bits of this and that in old lighthouse buildings, but you don't come here for the fixtures and fittings; its position across a giant chasm is wonderfully melodramatic.

And while you're down at this end, stop off for a seafood chowder at O'Sullivans on the quay in Crookhaven, Ireland's most southwesterly village. Crookhaven feels like a village in limbo, not really connected to the known world – an impression enhanced by the presence of disoriented French yachties who stagger along the quayside like drunkards, finding their land-legs after days at sea. Once upon a time this is where you would have heard the sonic boom as Concorde accelerated out over the Atlantic.

Mizen Head done, return up the peninsula to your overnight accommodation in Bantry House, which dominates the town of the same name. Owned by the eccentric, self-effacing, aristocratic Egerton Shelswell-White, whose trombone practise can be heard echoing down the hallways, this enormous 18th-century residence is plainly a struggle to maintain, but its library and gardens – particularly the wisteria around the fountains – are fabulous. Every June this is the setting for the West Cork Music Festival, for which your aristocratic host is the driving force.

Day two of your weekend is harder on your feet. Set off down the Sheep's Head peninsula, parallel to yesterday's drive down Mizen Head. Head down through Kilcrohane to Black Gate, turn right and cross over to above the cove at Gortavallig, where you can park your car. Then set off along the Sheep's Head Way, a well-signposted coastal path 55 miles long, of which you're just going to do the last handful of miles to the peninsula's tip.

Ninety minutes of wonderful scenery later – a chance of spotting dolphins or whales – and you'll reach the point, with its rather disappointing little lighthouse, built in the 1960s to guide supertankers. Look carefully downwards and you might spot tell-tale parallel ridges which indicate where the poorest of the poor, who couldn't afford to pay the rent on better land, desperately tried to grow potatoes. The slate-coloured lake just inland is Lough Akeen, said to be so deep that a farmer's horse which fell into the Lough actually emerged from the sea, several hundred feet below.

Round the point and head back northeast up a rising path and you'll reach a parking place with a static caravan, where Bernie Tobin serves tea and cakes to those that make it this far. If you ask her, Bernie will point out Odie the seagull, a bird that has become so fond of her cooking that she has to be careful to keep her car shut, to stop the bird clambering inside to investigate anything left on the back seat.

Bernie also regularly takes pity on exhausted walkers, shutting up shop to take them back to their cars. Hopefully you won't need that, now that you've got some of her cake.

PRACTICALITIES

GETTING THERE

Aer Lingus
☎ 0870 876 5000; *www.aerlingus.com*
Flies to Cork from Heathrow, expect to pay from £70 return.

TOURIST INFORMATION

Cork
☎ +353 21 425 5100; *www.corkkerry.ie, www.schull.ie, www.mizenhead.net*

CAR HIRE

Hire a car at Cork Airport from the likes of **Budget Ireland** (☎ +353 90 662 7711; *www.budget-ireland.com*), who charge around €25 a day.

ACCOMMODATION

Bantry House $ $ $ $
Bantry
☎ + 353 27 50 047; *www.bantryhouse.com*

WHERE TO EAT

Annie's Restaurant
Ballydehob
☎ +353 28 37 292

WALKING THE WACHAU

44

THERE'S A STRETCH OF THE DANUBE IN AUSTRIA
WHERE PICTURE POSTCARDS ARE MADE IN HEAVEN.
IT'S A STRETCH WHERE THE RIVERBANKS RISE UP,
TRESSED IN VINEYARDS, STUDDED WITH BAROQUE
CHURCHES AND TOPPED WITH CASTLES. IT'S ALSO THE
LAND OF THE HEURIGER — YOUNG WINE — WHICH CAN
SO EASILY WOBBLE THE KNEES OF AN UNWARY WALKER.

ALTHOUGH THE WACHAU OFFICIALLY BEGINS FURTHER
west, I suggest you start at Spitz, where the fruit
orchards and vineyards begin. This is also the
end station for the hourly train service from
Krems, whose route you will be effectively
retracing.

THE WACHAU

However if you are happy to walk a bit
more and choose your trains carefully,
you could go 5km further to Willendorf,
where a fertility figure from 25000BC was
discovered back in 1908 during the construction of the railway line.
The *Willendorf Venus*, as she is called, is a heavy-breasted, wide-
hipped statuette which a nomadic hunter probably kept by his
bedside. There's a large copy on the embankment above the railway
station, and the body shape is comfortingly maternal, the sort of
silhouette you might see running an Italian pizzeria anywhere along
the Adriatic coast.

Whether you start from Willendorf or Spitz the steep-sided
Wachau is easy to navigate and you can't really make a mistake with
your route; mostly it lies along lanes used by occasional tractors and
plenty of cyclists and is clearly waymarked.

Between Willendorf and Spitz the fruit orchards win the battle for
space, forcing the vines up onto ledges on the valley sides, but from

Spitz onwards the orchards are overwhelmed, and the whole valley becomes quilted with vineyards, most of them small and family owned. Each patch on that quilt has a little shed used by the vintner, and each is slightly differently orientated according to the vintner's whim. From afar it looks as if the vineyards are performing a stately waltz around reluctant wooden partners.

Spitz has a 15th-century *rathaus* (town hall) and a castle with a shipping museum, but frankly it is just as interesting to watch the real thing out on the water, struggling with one of the fastest-flowing stretches of the Danube. Some of the push-tugs and barges here will have come from as far away as the Ukraine (yellow and blue flags flying from the stern), and they'll be crawling along as slow as 4km/h as they push upstream.

Emerging from Spitz, look up to your left at the vine-clad hill called Tausendeimerberg, literally 'thousand bucket mountain', which in a good year is meant to produce 56,000 litres of wine. By now there'll be temptation all around you in the shape of Heuriger, which as well as denoting fresh young wine before it is bottled, is also the name given to the little family-run wine-gardens along the side of the road. These are often marked by bundles of straw, indicating that the family vintage is ready for consumption.

The most common grape variety here is the Gruner Veltiner, and you'll be asked whether you want an *achtel* or a *viertel*, an eighth or a quarter. We're talking litres, so if you want to keep on walking I'd recommend a *viertel*, even though it seems seductively refreshing at the time.

Only 6km on from Spitz is Weissenkirchen, a pretty place with a 16th-century Gothic church, and pleasantly uncrowded; you'll see what I mean by uncrowded when you've gone another 6km beyond that to Dürnstein, the village where all the cruise boats and the tour buses end up.

They come here for good reason; Dürnstein is tremendously attractive, located on a dramatic bend in the river, with a ruined castle up above where Richard the Lionheart was once incarcerated before being found by his faithful servant Blondel. Few of the cruise or bus passengers make it up the steep path to the castle ruins, whose wall-stubs flick V-signs in all directions. The view from up here is something else, particularly at the beginning or the end of the day, and to the east you can see as far as the hilltop monastery of Gottweig, the Austrian Montecassino.

Dürnstein's pretty big on shopping, eating and drinking, but it also has a very distinguished abbey, whose church has a fabulous, highly decorated blue belltower right by the riverside. With all its scrolls, pilasters, sculptures and gold leaf, the tower looks as if it has been fashioned out of delicate china, not stone.

For a brief while beyond Dürnstein the Wachau's vineyards swell in size and become more corporate and less mom-and-pop, with professional-looking wine-tasting venues and men on tractors talking to sales executives in suits. This is Unterloiben, really just a suburb of Dürnstein, and worth noting because it has a range of less expensive guesthouses than Dürnstein itself.

Then the valley narrows again and you're into Stein, a good-looking place were it not for its proximity to the busy road, and that in turn develops into Krems. This 1,000-year-old university town manages to be both ancient and lively, although it can seem a touch too frenetic for walkers who've got used to the leisurely rhythm of the Wachau.

PRACTICALITIES

GETTING THERE

Air Berlin (☎ *0871 500 0737; www.airberlin.com*) has flights from Stansted to Vienna from around £120 return.

From Vienna's Sudbahnhof there are frequent trains to Krems, where you need to change for the onward service to Spitz (hourly) or Willendorf (four a day); a total journey time of around 90 minutes. Austrian Railways (*www.oebb.at*).

If you want to return to Vienna via the river, the DDSG (*www.ddsg-blue-danube.at*) has a daily sailing leaving Dürnstein at 16.40 and Krems at 17.00 that'll bring you into Vienna for 21.00.

TOURIST INFORMATION

Austria

☎ *0845 101 1818; www.wachau.at*

ACCOMMODATION

Stockingerhof S S

☎ *+43 271 1384; www.stockingerhof.at*

Stay in family-owned winery and inn run by the Stockinger family, just out of the centre of Dürnstein.

Hotel Alte Post S

Krems

☎ *+43 273 282 276; www.alte-post.at*

For arriving and leaving, try this lovely old 18th-century building, which represents better value than anything you'll find in Vienna.

45

RUSSIAN-ABOUT IN NICE

IT WASN'T JUST THE BRITISH WHO PUT NICE ON THE
MAP, THE CITY WAS A FAVOURITE WITH RUSSIAN
ARISTOCRATS, TOO. VISIT THE CITY'S RUSSIAN
MANSIONS, CATHEDRAL AND GRAVEYARD. THERE'S
EVEN A PLACE FOR *BLINIS* AND *BORSCHT*.

ON A HILLSIDE IN LEAFY CAUCADE, WITHIN SPITTING
distance of Nice Airport, is the last home of
poets, princes, and countesses, all of them
Russian. These Lobanovs and Romanovs rest
under slabs of marble and in grand dynastic
tombs in the shade of a tumbling willow.
Some were unwilling exiles, and many
others originally came to the Côte D'Azur
for a bit of regal recreation 150 years ago,
and never managed to tear themselves
away.

   We British tend to take the credit for putting the resort of Nice on
the map, but it is fair to say that while our very own aristos-with-
cash may have made the first big entrance, Russian royalty was not
far behind. For much of the 19th century wave upon wave of
gentlefolk of both nations descended on the Riviera, sketching,
botanising and indulging in *soirées musicales*, and all for the sake of
their health. The coast has developed hugely since then, and
sketching and botanising has been replaced by gourmandising and
shopping, but it is still easy for a contemporary visitor to appreciate
what the gentry found so appealing about Nice.

   This is a wonderfully restorative place to be in the dead months
of the year, and it is only when you step out of the plane under these
bright-blue skies, to the scent of mimosa, the sight of fruit-laden
orange trees and the sound of water sprinklers still irrigating the

grass, do you realise quite how demoralising our northern European weather can be.

But it is not just the uplifting blues and golds, tastes and smells that make Nice a great weekend away, because both groups of original settlers have left a legacy of unusual landmarks.

The greatest work of the English was undoubtedly the Promenade des Anglais, one of Europe's most famous roads, which was the brainchild of the Reverend Lewis Way, vicar to the overwintering gentry. These days that Old Money has melted into the hills and the Promenade has become the haunt of joggers and roller-bladers, Italians and Japanese. Of course we *Anglais* are still very much in evidence too, still heading for hotels with names like Westminster and West End, but we arrive with a new type of horseless carriage with 'easyJet' painted on the side.

In the old days, while the English were busy with the Promenade, the Russians were taking on French mistresses and installing them in glorious *belle époque* villas, then salving their consciences by erecting one of the very few Russian cathedrals that exist outside the motherland.

The gleaming, onion-domed Saint Nicholas Cathedral on Boulevard Tsarevitch has to be one of Nice's biggest surprises, surrounded as it is by typically French mid-rise apartment complexes. It was built by the future Tsar Alexander III at the whim of his mother, in the dying throes of Imperial Russia. Inside is a wall of richly coloured icons hung with incense burners; outside you might see a pair of Russians waylay the black-robed priest, for a long, animated discussion. They're unlikely to be exiled aristocrats – more likely crew from Roman Abramovich's private yacht in port – and their conversation probably features the successes of Chelsea and Dynamo Kiev.

Within easy walking distance of the cathedral, down Avenue des Baumettes, is the hugely imposing former home of a Ukrainian princess – so imposing that it has since become the Fine Arts Museum, with a collection that reflects something of the Côte D'Azur's colours and light, through paintings by the likes of Dufy, Monet and Chéret.

Next door to that is a pink-walled castellated villa built in the shade of whispering pines by Prince Lobanov-Rostowsky, 150 years ago. Until recently this was called the Château des Ollieres, and was one of the most elegant small hotels in Nice until its aged owner died. The interiors are all original *chinoiseries* and stained glass, oil paintings, Meissen porcelain, taffeta and silk. A harpist used to play in the dining room at night and gave opera lessons behind closed doors by day. Old Money Russians used to frequent the Château, speaking French. These days the nouveau riche tend to congregate in New Money places like Cannes and Monte Carlo, and they don't bother to learn the language, although many of them attend charm school in Monaco to acquire the appropriate table manners for high society.

Any of today's Russians hankering after familiar food can head into Old Nice, the revitalised quarter around the flower market in Cours Saleya, which is full of farmers' wives selling herbs, honey and cheese. A little further inland is the remains of the old fish market, where gossiping fishmongers have been removing the bones from sardines for so long they no longer need to watch their hands while they do it. And between the two, down the tall, narrow streets filled with small handmade boutiques where sunlight bounds off ochre walls, is the Maison Russe: a good place for caviar, *blinis* and *borscht*, and for eavesdropping on Russian conversation. Also a good place for *pissaladière*, the rather un-appealingly named Nice equivalent of pizza.

Some Russians eventually returned home and Prince Lobanov-Rostowsky even became prime minister, albeit briefly. But the rest of the original émigrés never left; with the coming of the Revolution, they became the unacceptable face of the aristocracy. Many eventually died in Nice, to be interred in the Russian cemetery in leafy Caucade.

PRACTICALITIES

GETTING THERE

EasyJet

☎ *0905 821 0905; www.easyjet.com*

Frequent flights from Gatwick to Nice. Expect to pay from around £100 return.

TOURIST INFORMATION

French Tourist Office

☎ *0906 824 4123; www.franceguide.com*

Nice information

☎ *+ 33 4 92 14 46 28; www.nicetourism.com*

ACCOMMODATION

Hotel Felix $ $

Rue Massena

☎ *+33 4 93 88 67 73; www.hotel-felix-nice.federal-hotel.com*

Right in the pedestrian zone in the centre.

PLACES OF INTEREST

Fine Arts Museum

Avenue des Baumettes

☎ *+33 4 92 15 28 28; www.musee-beaux-arts-nice.org*

Cosy, cultural Ghent

46

The Belgians are good at doing cosy. Brown bars and strong beers help. Their cities are civilised and they're pretty handy at shop-window decoration too. Furthermore their nation doesn't get another entry in this book, despite being just across the water. So here is Ghent. Or Gent, Gand or Gando, depending where you're coming from.

Elbowed out of the tourist brochures by Bruges, its rather plump and prettified neighbour to the northwest, the city of Ghent is where modern and ancient Belgium collide. At its core it is just as pretty as Bruges can be, but it does have a large industrial hinterland, with the result that penetrating through to the cobbled centre is like stepping from a Cubist jungle into a market scene by Brueghel or Hieronymus Bosch.

  Ghent has the added advantage of not being Brussels, where every second person works for the EU and prices are massively inflated as a result. From Ghent's perspective, Brussels is an upstart. Back in the 12th century, this was the second-biggest city in Europe after Paris, and it has managed to get through successive European conflicts without getting too knocked about. At the same time, however, it has been too busy getting on with real life – this is Belgium's second port – to have become sanitised by tourism. Its gable ends are authentically crumbling, and its canals have a whiff of medieval waste arrangements. Moreover the people in town really

are Belgians, and not Eurocrats as in Brussels or coach parties from Birmingham, as in Bruges.

Locals here speak a ruddy form of Flemish – sounds more like phlegm-ish – that had to compete with the noise of clogs on cobbles, and still rings out loud and clear in the marketplaces. Once upon a time this language was limited to the kitchens of big houses, with French the polite language spoken above stairs. But then the balance of power changed and these days you hear only French spoken in Ghent's opera house or in one of the city's very posh pâtisseries.

Language and gritty outskirts apart, this is a dreamy place lined with boutiques lavishly stocked with the luxuries of life. And when window shopping palls, you can always retreat to the carved, panelled interior of the Tempelier, just off the Vrijdagmarkt, to worship Belgian beer. On quiet nights the landlady will challenge you to backgammon.

The city's colourful history is of warrior-traders sweeping through in a swirl of architectural styles – Romanesque, Gothic, Brabant Gothic and Italian Renaissance – and they have given Ghent a fierce sense of its own independence. Ghent Castle's Gravensteen looks like a film set from *Arabian Nights*, but it was not built for traditional purposes of self-defence: it was a threat to keep the uppish burghers in their place.

Downtown the city is an encyclopaedia of northern European architecture, with gable ends all the way from Romanesque to Brabant Gothic, particularly in the row of waterside façades on the Graslei. In the winter gloom it all looks fabulous, but a bit of dampness underfoot can turn the cobbles into bars of soap, so beware.

And then there are Ghent's three massive towers in a row: St Nicholas Church, the Belfry and the Cathedral, all erected piecemeal from the 11th century onwards. A pretty handy way for city merchants to keep an eye on their shipping on the converging rivers Leie and Scheldt, not to mention all the God-bothering business.

St Bavo's Cathedral is an eclectic mix of architectural styles, but its key attraction is a treasure of an altarpiece by the brothers Van Eyck kept in a side chapel: the *Mystic Lamb*. This 15th-century painting is thought to include the first ever life-modelled nudes. The detail is remarkable; with a magnifying glass one can identify 42 different wild flowers. Originally kept closed during the week, the painting would send a ripple of pleasure through the congregation when it was opened.

It has certainly had a colourful life. During a period of extreme Calvinism the nudes were clothed and the painting was hidden in the tower; Napoleon removed it to the Louvre, the side panels ended up in Berlin after World War I and the whole thing was found in the Pyrenees after World War II.

Elsewhere, Ghent's cultural attractions are as much modern as ancient. Inland, in the Museum of Fine Arts in Citadel Park, there are rooms rich with the Brueghelesque details of life, the baking, the drinking and the clog-hopping festivals. Meanwhile across the way is SMAK, the modern art collection, with contemporary creativity at its most arresting, from the wall doodles by someone who signed herself HFA (Happy Female Artist) to the room titled 'Young and depressed in Scandinavia'.

If you've got the time and the inclination, there's an excellent out-of-town artistic trail to be made to the villages of Deurle and Sint-Martens-Latem. On weekends in season you can travel by boat up the Leie; otherwise take the 75b bus. The Sint-Martens movement flourished just after the turn of the 20th century, was largely Expressionist and concentrated on figures in a landscape. Of the three galleries, the most comprehensive collection is in the Dhondt-Dhaenens. But you don't have to be an arts buff to enjoy being here. The attraction is the setting, gracious living in a typical landscape of slow river, pollarded trees and ploughed fields. And a good array of bars and restaurants from which to enjoy it all.

PRACTICALITIES

GETTING THERE

Eurostar to Brussels, frequent onward connections to Ghent (☏ *0870 442 8951; www.eurostar.com*). Fares to Brussels from £99 return.

TOURIST INFORMATION

Belgium
www.visitbelgium.com
Ghent
☏ *+32 92 66 56 60; www.visitgent.be*

ACCOMMODATION

Best Western Cour Saint-Georges (Sint Jorishof) $ $ $
☏ *+32 92 24 24 24; www.courstgeorges.be*
Historic hotel right in the centre.
A really interesting range of small, personal and stylish hotels and B&Bs can be found on *www.weekendhotel.be*.

PLACES OF INTEREST

Museum of Fine Arts
☏ *+32 92 40 07 00; www.mskgent.be*
SMAK
☏ *+32 92 21 17 03; www.smak.be*
's Gravensteen
☏ *+32 92 25 93 06*

INDUSTRIAL SAFARI IN THE RUHR

47

THE RUHR VALLEY IS NO TRADITIONAL HOLIDAY HOTSPOT. THIS INDUSTRIAL HINTERLAND MAKES A DREAM WEEKEND FOR THE RUST FAMILY, PERHAPS: AN ADVENTURE BREAK FOR METAL FATIGUE, OR A GOOD PLACE FOR SLAG TO GO CAMPING. AND YET SOME OF ITS MINES, FURNACES AND STEEL MILLS HAVE HAD A MAKEOVER, AND NOW THE RUHR IS GOING TO BE EUROPEAN CAPITAL OF CULTURE FOR 2010. COAL MINES CAN BE BEAUTIFUL, TOO.

THERE'S NOTHING CONVENTIONALLY ATTRACTIVE ABOUT the Ruhrgebiet. This is Germany's hairy armpit. The land is flat, the rivers murky. Cities like Essen, Dortmund, Duisburg and Gelsenkirchen merge into each other, all of them assembled out of large blocks, some from the 1920s, but most from the 1950s onwards thanks to 'redevelopment' by the RAF during World War II. And so to come here as a tourist requires opening one's eyes and one's mind to something a bit different, to a form of human endeavour that makes the pyramids seem piddly by comparison: German heavy industry.

RUHR VALLEY

Not so long ago there were 140 coal mines and scores of associated blast furnaces and steel mills in this region. Huge quantities of imported labour were required to work these giants, with four million people moving into the area from the mid 19th to early 20th century. But now, 100 years later, the global economy has changed, and there are only seven operational mines left.

However the region has not been left to rot. Local government, federal government and the EU have dug deep into their pockets to attract new kinds of enterprise and to fund the conversion of many industrial dinosaurs into new recreational cathedrals. Apart from

creating employment, the idea has been to bring back a sense of self-respect to the area, to make people feel proud of what their fathers and grandfathers achieved.

And so, these days, you can go to an art gallery in the world's second-largest gasometer; you can ride a big dipper in the world's most beautiful coal mine; you can attend a blockbuster musical in the workshop of the world's largest steel maker and you can stroll around a country park which was once an ironworks, but which now hosts (amongst other things) Europe's biggest indoor diving centre. All of which used to be forbidden territory.

And while you're there, you can stay in a hotel which was once a coal mine's wage-hall (see *Practicalities* below).

The most high-profile of the transformed industries is the 'beautiful' coal mine, Zeche Zollverein, near Essen. Recognised as a World Heritage Site by UNESCO back in 2001, the brick-built and Bauhaus-inspired mine looks like a Frank Lloyd Wright château, and is stuffed with museums and galleries. A long walkway across a wasteland of cinders fast disappearing under a forest of birch leads to the Kokerie Zollverein, where coal dust was fire-blasted into industrial carbon (coke) which burns hot enough to melt metal. Here a big dipper and a swimming pool have been set amongst the ovens and you can wander down the evacuated smoke chambers to stare up a huge chimney to the orb of daylight a giddy 300ft overhead.

There's more creativity on display over at the gasometer at Oberhausen, now a giant art gallery whose exhibitions have to be tailor made to fit. It seems that artists are queuing up to have a go –

Reichstag-wrapper Christo was one of the first – at creating something that makes proper use of such a huge vertical space. From the top, 118m up, there's a 360° view of Lowry-like spires and smoke stacks. (There were slag heaps too, but many have been sold off to the Netherlands for land reclamation.)

The gasometer has to cover its costs by seeking sponsorship, one of few Ruhr sites which doesn't survive on some form of subsidy. Also standing on its own two feet is the Colosseo Theatre in Essen, in a huge rectangular building which was once Krupp's mechanical workshop. All the building's original structure has been retained, even down to the gantry cranes across the roof, but encased inside it is a lavish auditorium where top-end musicals – *Phantom of the Opera*, *Mamma Mia*, etc – are staged. Worth visiting for the foyer alone.

In the end the most user-friendly of all these sites is the Landschaftspark Duisburg-Nord, a clunky old name for a clunky old place.

Duisburg-Nord is a former ironworks with towers, gasometers, bunkers, silos, crucibles, power plants and compressor rooms, all on an immense scale – and many now with new uses, since closure in 1985. Bits are tarted up: the compressor room hosts dinners and weddings; the gasometer is filled with water for the indoor diving centre, the massive concrete bunkers have been turned into climbing walls, furnace number five has been dedicated to mountaineers, and an open-air cinema with a rolling roof has been inserted into furnace number one.

Outside, the buddleia has been encouraged to run wild in the parkland, and there are sufficient cycle tracks on the remaining slag heaps to stage a 24-hour mountain-bike race. And when darkness falls the whole tangled mass turns into a living, looming thing thanks to British lighting designer Jonathan Park.

These and the other 20-odd locations on Ruhr's Industrial Heritage Trail represent remarkable lateral thinking in an era that still regards industrial buildings as a blot on the landscape. A grippingly good industrial safari amongst slag, rust and metal fatigue.

P R A C T I C A L I T I E S

GETTING THERE

The Ruhr is six hours' drive from the Channel ports. The best air access is via Dusseldorf. **Air Berlin** (☏ *0871 500 0737; www.airberlin.com*) has flights from Stansted; expect to pay around £100 return. From Dusseldorf Airport there are trains every 15 minutes to Essen, gateway city to the Ruhr. All industrial sites are reachable by public transport; enquire locally.

TOURIST INFORMATION

Germany Tourist Board
☏ *020 7317 0908; www.germany-tourism.co.uk*
Ruhrgebiet (Ruhr Valley) Tourism
☏ *+49 20 117 671 22; www.ruhrgebiettouristik.de*
The website *www.route-industriekultur.de* has details of key locations.

ACCOMMODATION

Alte Lohnhalle $ $
Rotthauser Strasse, Essen
☏ *+49 20 138 4570; www.Alte-Lohnhalle.de*
Funky design in old coal mine building, with a defunct pit head next door.

GO TO SEA FOR
A SHILLING

48

THE CHEAPEST FORM OF CRUISING, PARTICULARLY
NOW THE HOLIDAY SEASON IS OVER, IS TO TAKE A
BERTH ON ONE OF THE LONG-HAUL FERRIES TO
EUROPE OR SCANDINAVIA. AT JUST £39 RETURN, THE
DFDS SERVICE FROM NEWCASTLE TO AMSTERDAM IS
ONE OF THE MOST INEXPENSIVE WEEKENDS IN THE
WHOLE TOURISM INDUSTRY.

SHORT-HAUL FERRY CROSSINGS (IE: DOVER–CALAIS
etc) give the wrong impression of ferry travel,
being more an exercise in retailing than anything
else. The food is fast, the lighting is neon and
everything is vulcanised and washable, in case
of sickness. And as for those catamaran
fast ferries – aka vomit rockets – that is
transport, not travel.

MINI-CRUISING

Long-haul journeys are rather different.
There's something womb-like about these
ferries in autumn, particularly the sensation of being rocked gently in
your berth at night to the distant thrum of engines. Out there,
through the specially toughened glass, the elements are doing their
worst; in here it's warm, the cinemas have the latest releases, there's
a choice of restaurants, the drink is cheap, and there's plenty of
comfy seating to curl up with a good book in advance of the
evening's disco. I'd even recommend it as a place to take yourself off
to finish a big piece of work, provided the weather doesn't cut up
rough. And if you're interested in a journey's eco-credentials,
travelling by ferry means that you're not making much more than a
pinprick in the ozone layer.

You may not have noticed how these longer-distance ferries have
been going steadily upmarket if you've been using the Channel Tunnel

or low-cost airlines. Some of them now have celebrity-chef restaurants; most have an on-board band – usually of Bulgarians – which hammer out creditable cover versions of old favourites, and many have casinos. Some even have swimming pools, notably the *Pont Aven*, which runs the Plymouth to Santander route for Brittany Ferries, although I doubt that you'll find these pools particularly restful at this time of year. For example heading out on the *Pont Aven* over the Bay of Biscay, one of the world's most reliable wave machines, you'd be in danger of being thrown out of the bathwater with the baby if the crew didn't cover the pool with netting when the ship began to roll.

Four routes are worth considering for this autumn mini-cruising, on the basis that they satisfy the criteria for convenient departure and arrival times, distance and style of ship.

Portsmouth to St Malo with Brittany Ferries is a good one. The restaurant – crisp linen and *fruit de mer* – on the MV *Bretagne* provides a wonderful vantage point from which to watch the lights of Portsmouth and the Isle of Wight disappear steadily astern.

Unless you're desperate for nightlife, this 12-hour journey is a touch too short for staying up late. In any case you'll want to be up early to witness the arrival at St Malo, a wonderful, circular, walled city which looms out of the sea mist. One of the most charismatic of all French Channel ports.

Harwich to Esbjerg with DFDS is a longer voyage – 19 hours or so – and its convenient tea-time departure from Harwich provides a balcony view of the busy container port of Felixstowe as you glide slowly through. As darkness falls the ship will be out in a seascape dotted with North Sea Oil platforms, glowing like torches through the dark.

The MV *Dana Sirena* has two restaurants, one with *smorgasbord*, a Scandinavian buffet dinner where you can eat as much as you like, and the other a more formal *à la carte*. Unusually, this ship has in-cabin televisions with movie channels instead of on-board cinema.

Esbjerg itself is, frankly, dull. But you don't have much time to spend there before the ship sets off back again.

Plymouth to Santander with Brittany Ferries is another long one (18 hours), although the MV *Pont Aven* fairly flies across the Bay of

Biscay. This is the ferry with the pool, the on-board wine tastings, a useful tourism office, a couple of cinemas, and a choice of French restaurants, as well as *tapas* up by the pool and the chance of seeing a few whales, which the captain will usually point out. At peak times you can even have Spanish lessons on board.

As a destination, Santander has got far more going for it than Esbjerg, or even grimy old Bilbao, the other ferry alternative to Spain. It has an elegant old historic port district, sizeable outlying beaches that are favourite weekend destinations for *madrileños* escaping the summer heat, and the ferry berth is right in the centre.

And finally, **Newcastle to Amsterdam with DFDS** is both convenient and extremely good value. Ships leave daily, at handy times, viz 17.30 from Newcastle and 18.00 from Amsterdam, and arrive at equally handy times, viz 09.30 in Amsterdam and 09.00 in Newcastle. From the ferry port at Ijmuiden (some distance out) there's a bus laid on to take you direct to Amsterdam's Central Station, and you'll pretty much get there just as all the museums, strip clubs and head shops are opening for business.

Amsterdam's easy-breezy reputation combined with the ease (and low price) of the DFDS crossing means that the ships tend to fill up, and can be quite raucous at weekends. Besides the normal cocktail lounge etc, both vessels have a sports bar and a karaoke bar, to cater for those looking for a good time. If you do go for the mini-cruise with the day in Amsterdam, I suspect you'll find the return trip considerably quieter, unless modern stag and hen parties have a lot more stamina than they used to!

PRACTICALITIES

GETTING THERE

DFDS

❩ *0870 252 0524; www.dfdsseaways.co.uk*

Return mini-cruise Harwich to Esbjerg from £64 per person and Newcastle to Amsterdam from £39, cabin included, based on two sharing.

Brittany Ferries

❩ *0870 536 0360; www.brittany-ferries.com*

Return mini-cruise Portsmouth to St Malo from £75 per person and Plymouth to Santander from £79, cabin included, based on two sharing. Note that both companies decrease the number of sailings towards the end of the year.

49

SAN MARINO'S TOP SHOP
REPUBLIC

PRE-CHRISTMAS SHOPPING IN SAN MARINO. THE
WORLD'S OLDEST SURVIVING REPUBLIC HAS ONE OF
THOSE NAMES THAT COULD BE ANYTHING FROM A
TYPE OF TOILET CLEANER TO A LOST EMPIRE. PERCHED
ON A HILLTOP IN THE MIDDLE OF ITALY, IT OWES ITS
ORIGINS TO A PIOUS HERMIT AND ITS PROSPERITY TO
TAX BREAKS.

THERE'S HARDLY A BETTER EXAMPLE OF HOW SPORT
can put a country on the map than San Marino.
Many of you will know of its name either
because of its Grand Prix (which doesn't
actually take place here at all, but in Imola in
Italy) or because of its football team, who
regularly pop up for a ritual drubbing in
the early rounds of European
competitions.

In a nation with a total population of
26,000 – a quarter of the size of Basingstoke – and whose
location is a mystery to most of us, a natural athlete is a busy
chap. San Marino's foremost sprinter was recently unable to make
the World Championships thanks to a double booking with his
tennis career, and its football manager is a part-time PE teacher in
a local primary school. However, playing in the international arena
is not about winning, but about being San Marino's ambassadors-
with-dirty-knees, putting the republic's name out and about. Mind
you, the football team did make a bit of a splash when they scored
a goal within the opening minute of a match against England
some years ago.

However sport is not the only thing that puts this tiny state on the
map. It has history, shopping, a great view, and (in case you didn't

know) it rises right next to Rimini, the fashionable resort on the Italian Adriatic.

Actually, more correctly, it rises 15 miles inland, atop brooding Monte Titano, girdled by post-Modernist shopping centres and crowned by 14th-century castles. Its walled summit is crammed with medieval streets, guarded by an army of 65 volunteers with feathers in their helmets. An arms dealer who knew nothing about the tiny republic recently offered these feather-wearing militia a cheap deal on intercontinental missiles, after coming across San Marino on the internet. Needless to say, no purchases were made, and the state's only military manoeuvres are during Independence Day (3 September) when soldiers and incomers take part in a crossbow competition all over town.

It may be tiny (60km²) but San Marino is no tin-pot dictatorship. Per-capita income is considerably higher than in Italy, car ownership is an astonishing 2.8 vehicles for every inhabitant, and everyone owns their own houses. Many a neighbouring Italian would dearly like to live here, and 5,000 drive in every day to work in the shops, hotels and restaurants.

It wasn't always thus. Originally founded back in AD301 by the followers of a pious hermit, it was granted sanctity by Papal decree, and even Napoleon left it alone. During World War II it kept its neutrality and thereby played host to 100,000 refugees from Italian fascism, but otherwise during the 20th century it had a hard time keeping its citizens – there was a big emigration to America – until tourism came to stay in the 1960s.

Initially the state's stamps and coins – collectors' items – became major sources of revenue, but then the concept of duty free took hold, and San Marino realised that it had a big future in luxury shopping. Today, advertising for factory outlets, much of it in Russian, covers the arrival halls at Rimini Airport. Up on Monte Titano the steep narrow streets glitter with jewellery, alcohol, and perfume shops, with gaudy glassware, obscure liqueurs, and a peculiar line in replica guns. Down on Monte Titano's skirts below are new malls crammed with electronics, fur coats, shoes and clothes.

To label these items 'duty free' would not be quite accurate in today's European market, despite them being free of Italy's 20%

sales tax. Most prices include a local tax of around 4%, but the shopkeepers point out that direct importation from the manufacturers also considerably reduces costs.

For foreigners, the main bargain is not in the electronics or the fridge-freezers, but in the Italian goods – especially the factory outlets for the fashion houses, places like Grandi Griffe. Here you'll find the likes of Moschino, Valentino, Ungaro, GianFranco Ferre and Amerigo Vespucci, at accessible prices. I am not the world's best shopper, but even I know that £80 is a snip for a designer-label wool suit.

All this mammon-like activity is well away down the switchback road from the elegant old hilltop, where the peaceful, refined atmosphere is for more uplifting thoughts – and a remarkable outlook, inevitably over foreign lands.

If there was ever any justification for invading San Marino it would not be for the shopping, nor for the rather paltry waxworks and torture museum up at the top of the hill: it would be for the view. On one side, the hills of Emilia Romagna. On the other, the sweep down to Rimini and the Adriatic, and on a clear night sometimes the lights of Venice and even the coast of Croatia.

As darkness falls the republic empties of tourists, the switchback road through the malls looking like an outpouring of neon vomit. It is worth staying up on Monte Titano for the sense of history and peace that returns to the hilltop cobbled streets, just as it does to Mont St Michel (see *weekend 7*).

In the morning, low-lying wraparound mist turns Monte Titano into a fairytale castellation in its own territory rising above the clouds. It's a place to think about birth, death, sex and taxation, although not necessarily in that order.

PRACTICALITIES

GETTING THERE

EasyJet (☏ *0905 821 0905; www.easyjet.com*) has flights from Luton for around £100 return, and **Ryanair** (☏ *0871 246 0000; www.ryanair.com*) flies from East Midlands Airport. Direct buses link downtown Rimini and San Marino, or take a taxi from the airport (around €30).

TOURIST INFORMATION

☏ *+37 8549 885430; www.visitsanmarino.com*

ACCOMMODATION

Hotel Rosa S S
Monte Titano
☏ *+37 8549 991961; www.hotelrosasanmarino.com*

SHOPPING

Factory outlet **Grandi Griffe**
www.smfactoryoutlet.com

50

HAPPY CHRISTMAS NUREMBERG

TO NUREMBERG, FOR AN UNLIKELY COMBINATION OF
CHRISTMAS SPIRIT AND A SHARP REMINDER OF MAN'S
INHUMANITY TO MAN. THE CITY OF NAZI RALLIES
AND WAR TRIALS HAS A GRUELLING, STIMULATING
'DOCUMENTATION CENTRE' IN THE FORMER RALLY
GROUNDS, AS WELL AS ONE OF THE MOST
COMPELLINGLY PRETTY CHRISTMAS MARKETS IN THE
WHOLE OF GERMANY.

HITLER'S NUREMBERG RALLIES AND THE POSTWAR
Nuremberg trials tend to define this city's image
in the eyes of the world, but most Germans know
Nuremberg for something far, far more innocent.
The nation's first ever Christmas Market started
here back in 1628, and it still stars a golden-
tressed Christ Child (*Kristkind*) and several
thousand *Zwetschgenmannle* – men made
out of prunes.

First impressions are of a steepled,
domed and gabled place, the colour of freshly baked pottery, set on
rippling hills that rise up ultimately to the Kaiserburg. From the
12th–16th centuries, the Kaiserburg was the residence of Holy Roman
Emperors, and the city was regarded as the empire's unofficial
capital. In those days the view from the Kaiserburg was probably not
too dissimilar to today, and there's very little to hint at Nuremberg's
very muddied recent history – or even to the fact that 90% of the old
city was destroyed by bombs one January morning in 1945. Virtually
the whole place has been painstakingly reconstructed as it once was,
with new and old building work woven carefully together. The net
result is very attractive, and it looks like it has been recently cleaned.

The old city is surrounded by walls anchored by regular, macho, hairy-chested barrel towers. Inside, the centre is largely pedestrian, on either side of a swirly river, with buskers along the walls and cobbles underfoot; this is meant to be the largest car-free centre in Europe. In the summer, there are tables and chairs all along these streets as shoppers get on the outside of serious coffee and cake. But now that it's the month before Christmas, attention is focused on the Hauptmarket, on the river's north bank.

This is home to the Christmas Market, with 200 stalls in wall-to-wall kitsch; carved houses with lights inside, glass tears, cheeky reindeer going ice-skating, handpainted tree decorations, music boxes with skating scenes, etc. 'Cherubs, Sir? How about half-a-dozen. You can never have enough cherubs in the house.'

Particular specialities are Nuremberg's *Lebkuchen*, those soft, circular cinnamon-and-gingerbread biscuits, often with a crust of chocolate. *Lebkuchen* come in as many different packagings as there are days in the year, but ultimately they all taste pretty similar. Then there are the prune-men, who are actually made out of several varieties of dried fruit and also come in many guises, from prune bank manager to prune dustman; you're meant to build up a collection.

Glühwein flows from every corner and is served in clay mugs that you're also meant to take home for your personal collection. If the *glühwein* begins to turn your knees to jelly, then it's time for Nuremberg sausages, which are supposed to be so small that they can be passed through a keyhole, although I'm not sure why you'd want to do that with a sausage. There's no point in thinking a) of your waistline or b) of staying off the booze, if you find yourself in Nuremberg at Christmas time.

The Market casts a spell on the place. Its emphasis is on a traditional Christmas for children, with the *Kristkind* (Christ Child), a golden-robed Rapunzel, making regular appearances in front of the 14th-century Frauenkirche, whose clock re-enacts the Homage of the Seven Electors to Emperor Charles IV every day at noon. Even when the *Kristkind* is not in attendance there are bound to be angels all in white, handing out sachets of something-or-other promotional. In the evenings the streets fill with processions of local kids holding homemade paper lanterns. Their excitement is infectious, and it doesn't take many *glühweins* to get a deep sense of peace and goodwill to all men.

However, and it is a big however, this isn't all there is to Nuremberg. Because of its Imperial past, Adolf Hitler chose to revive the city's tradition as the capital of the Reich. He built huge rally grounds just outside the old city, a prison-palace in brutalist style with echoes of Mayan temples and Roman colossea. It was meant to impress and intimidate, to perpetuate the mythology of the man. The first rally took place here in 1927, and thereafter Hitler came here every year to shriek at his adoring audience.

Much of the Rally Ground is still there, and it now houses a Documentation Centre, a very dry name for an outstanding exhibition which looks at the techniques employed by a megalomaniac to hijack a whole nation. His rallies were a key ingredient; they lasted up to eight days and inculcated a kind of group hysteria which is disturbing to witness, and probably all too easy to repeat: you don't think too much about what you're doing when everyone else is doing it too.

Hitler chose Nuremberg because it was the 'most German of all German cities'. That phrase may sound innocent enough, but it has an unpleasant resonance for the older generation, because in Nazi hands the idea carried a subtext of exclusion, domination, persecution and suppression; if you were not of the 'preferred race', then there was no place for you here in this 'most German' of places.

The exhibition skates across the war itself, and then deals with the war crimes tribunal which took place here afterwards, complete with film of Hermann Goering denying everything. It was the first time in human history that politicians were made answerable for decisions taken on an international stage. A practice, and a principle, which still causes controversy in the modern world.

PRACTICALITIES

GETTING THERE

Air Berlin
☏ *0871 500 0737; www.airberlin.com*
Flies from Stansted. Expect to pay upwards of £80 return.

TOURIST INFORMATION

Germany Tourist Board
☏ *020 7317 0908; www.germany-tourism.co.uk,*
www.tourismus-nuernberg.de.

ACCOMMODATION

Hotel Astoria `$ $`
Weidenkellerstrasse
☏ *+49 91 1208 505; www.hotel-astoria-nuernberg.de*

PLACES OF INTEREST

Rally Ground and Documentation Centre
www.museen-nuernberg.de
Christmas Market
www.christkindlesmarkt.de

51

CAPE BRETON'S CELTIC COLOURS

A FLING ON THE CAPE. NEW ENGLAND MAY GET ALL
THE PUBLICITY FOR FABULOUS AUTUMN COLOURS,
BUT THOSE COLOURS ARE JUST AS FINE IN NOVA
SCOTIA, AS WELL AS BEING CONSIDERABLY CLOSER.
ADDITIONALLY, CAPE BRETON HAS A FASCINATING
SCOTTISH COMMUNITY AND ONE OF THE BEST CELTIC
MUSIC FESTIVALS IN CHRISTENDOM, TIMED TO TAKE
PLACE WITH NATURE'S OWN DISPLAY.

AT THE BEGINNING OF THE 19TH CENTURY MOST
of the new settlers on Canada's eastern
seaboard spoke Gaelic. Most were refugees,
evicted from their homelands in Scotland by
big landlords who had decided to replace
their tenant farmers with sheep, in what
later became known as the Highland
Clearances.

So dominant did the Gaelic language
become in Nova Scotia – new Scotland –
that even the locally hired hands learned to speak it. The story goes
that one Highland lady, disembarking after her Atlantic crossing,
turned when she overheard her language being spoken on the wharf
to find that these Gaelic speakers were startlingly un-Celtic to look
at. 'Oh God of mercy,' she exclaimed, 'are we all going to turn black
like that?'

Nowhere was the concentration of Gaels higher than in Cape
Breton, an island the size of Cyprus linked by a narrow peninsula to
the mainland. Between 1815 and 1838 some 22,000 emigrants
shipped across to settle here, swiftly recreating the lifestyle they had
left, clearing space amongst the forests to pursue the same mix of

CAPE BRETON'S CELTIC COLOURS

fishing and farming. And because they were mostly illiterate, they created a strong culture of music and dance to recall their homeland.

Fast forward to the present day, and the Scottishness of Cape Breton doesn't immediately hit you between the eyes. Ukrainians dominate Sydney, its unappealing big city; some of its more attractive seaboard townships are French-speaking Acadian; inland there are Mi'kmaq (Native Indian) reserves, where the pastors chant in Latin from loudhailers on the top of Mission churches.

With all these languages cannoning around the Cape it is a challenge to pick out the Gaelic speakers, particularly as they tend to only speak it at home. But you start to encounter Scots as the land begins to steepen towards the north, where tartan galleries appear on the roadside next to Presbyterian churches and tea shops selling porridge bread. These places called Portree, Dunvegan and Inverness are still lived in by MacPhersons, MacPhees and MacNeils.

Nor is the feeling of *déjà vu* confined to names on a map. Northern Cape Breton, particularly that part lassoed by a 200-mile Cabot Trail (the eponymous navigator was the first European to touch ground here) is a raw mix of gunmetal water and uncompromising land typical of the Highlands, rising from a wild coastline to wind-seared bog and rock. This is great hiking country.

Come here in early October and these small communities fill with US-accented voices claiming to be '100% Scotch', and they don't mean they're all whisky. They're here for the annual Celtic Colours Festival, during which Cape Breton's Scottishness reaches fever pitch. The festival coincides with a slow-burn firework display from the forests of maple, oak and birch, where the trees seem to be playing their part in the festivities, simulating every colour of every tartan ever made.

Celtic Colours has become something of an annual pilgrimage for descendants of the original settlers of the Cape, many of whom have long since moved on further into mainland America. Although few sound remotely Scottish, they return to remember their roots, and they'll know all the words to all the Gaelic songs, which they sing with great emotional intensity. It is a strange feeling, sitting in village halls listening to massed voices singing word-perfectly in a language practically no-one understands.

Nova Scotia has its own high-quality core of Celtic musicians, who play at local ceilidhs throughout the year. For the festival, this local talent is supplemented with imported top performers from Scotland, Ireland, Brittany and northern Spain, and distributed to community centres and halls all over the island. Just finding the venues is something of a travel epic, particularly at nightfall in rural areas where the roads are busy with rutting moose. For this is the season when a male moose feels an irresistible urge, and he doesn't mind telling everyone about it.

It's not all back lanes, however. The festival is headquartered at the quiet town of Baddeck, and has a Festival Club rather like the Fringe Club at the Edinburgh Festival, where impromptu performances are likely to break out at any time.

Only around 500 residents of Cape Breton still speak Gaelic, but great efforts are being made to stop the language dying out altogether. The College of Celtic Arts and Crafts at St Ann's, the only Gaelic-medium college outside Scotland, organises language teaching in selected schools and does its best to preserve the traditions of music and dance. It has exhibitions about the first landings, which are quite a story in themselves, and it usually has some sort of residential course at festival time, mixing Gaelic lessons, bagpiping, whisky tastings and a dinner of mackerel and tatties.

The year I was there, there were supposed to be 19 Nigerians on that course. Sadly, this was not evidence of a Celtic resurgence in Africa, but a testament to the ingenuity of Nigerians when it comes to getting exit visas. Needless to say, none of them actually turned up.

PRACTICALITIES

GETTING THERE

Canadian Affair (☎ *020 7616 9184; www.canadianaffair.com*) has some of the best-value flights to Halifax, from around £200 return.
More choice of timings with **Air Canada** (☎ *0871 220 1111; www.aircanada.com*), but prices from £400 return.

TOURIST INFORMATION

☎ *0870 380 0070; www.canadatravel.ca*
Destination Cape Breton
www.cbisland.com

CAR HIRE

From Halifax Airport with **Argus Rentals** (☎ *020 7099 3787; www.argusrentals.com*) from around £25 per day.

ACCOMMODATION

Normaway Inn $ $
Margaree
☎ *+1 902 248 2987; www.normaway.com*
A rustic place run by emigrant Scots reminiscent of a Scottish country hotel.

FESTIVALS

For information on **Celtic Colours**, which usually takes place in the first week of October (☎ *+1 902 562 6700; www.celtic-colours.com*).

COURSES

Celtic College
St Ann's
www.gaeliccollege.edu

52

NEPAL WITHOUT THE LONG HAUL

THE KASBAH DU TOUBKAL IS A BRITISH/BERBER CO-
OPERATION IN MOROCCO'S ATLAS MOUNTAINS, AND
THE WINNER OF A CLUTCH OF ECOTOURISM AWARDS.
THE KASBAH WAS THE FORTIFIED HOME OF AN
ARISTOCRAT, AND IT SITS A DONKEY RIDE UP FROM
THE ROAD END, BELOW MOUNT TOUBKAL.

YOU MAY NOT RECOGNISE THE NAME KASBAH DU
Toubkal, but there's a good chance you will have
seen its picture. The building perches like an
eagle's nest on a rocky balcony below snow-
topped Mount Toubkal, the highest mountain
in north Africa at 4,165m. Roads have
penetrated the valley below as far as Imlil,
but the kasbah can still only be reached
by a short, steep climb either on foot or
on the back of a donkey.

● ATLAS
MOUNTAINS

   There's no machinery beyond the road end. The Berbers who live
up here pursue a traditional existence, relying on their own goats
and corn-crop terraces, and only travelling as far as their own legs
will carry them. Theirs is a distinct mountain culture very
reminiscent of the Himalayas, with perched villages, mule trains,
and back-breaking subsistence living.

   The simplicity of that existence, the magnificence of the scenery
and the purity of the air attracts increasing numbers of visitors,
and you can see why. Walking along these precipitous paths is
like going trekking in Nepal, but without having to fly halfway
round the world – and risk Maoist guerillas – to do so. In fact
these mountains are regularly passed off as the Himalayas on the
big screen, most recently when the kasbah played the part of a

Tibetan monastery in *Kundun*, Martin Scorsese's film about the Dalai Lama.

The kasbah is the former summer residence of a Glaoui Caid, a local chief, although it has been much altered. It describes itself as a 'Berber hospitality centre' rather than a hotel, and is a joint project between British former schoolteacher Mike McHugo, now resident in France, who started to bring school groups here many years ago, working with local guide Haji Maurice, one of his first contacts in the mountains. It's good to see something with solid eco-credentials doing very nicely, thank you. Proof that you don't have to have a big PR machine to thrive.

The journey up to the kasbah from Marrakesh, the closest big city, takes 90 minutes, and *en route* passes another British project with considerably more snob value: Richard Branson's Kasbah de Tamadot. Tamadot is the ultimate in luxury, complete with infinity pool and the only fitness centre in the Atlas Mountains. Mind you, there's a fair case for saying that the mountains are a bit of a fitness centre in themselves, and they come free of charge, but Branson's guests are unlikely to venture far from their spa to test them out.

Not that Kasbah du Toubkal is particularly primitive. It has half-a-dozen bedrooms and a couple of suites, all equipped with the likes of CD players, black soap, local shampoo ('mud for the hairs') and a suitable range of Moroccan clothes if you want to go native. Décor is an eclectic mixture of Ikea and Berber, stone, tile and walnut, and one of the suites even has an open log fire in winter.

As the 'hospitality centre' tag suggests, the atmosphere is

informal, and there's a strong feeling of community, although it is diminished during the day when the kasbah's roof-terracing becomes a popular luncheon place for daytrippers, who can't resist the view.

A large proportion of the overnighting clientele is British, come to take the mountain air. In the evenings everyone gathers for dinner in the log-fired dining area and swaps notes on their day's adventures – how they'd joined in with a group of children playing football on a mountain track, how they'd rented a mule for a handful of euros a day, and how they'd watched the village girls returning in the evening virtually invisible under giant bundles of foliage, like giant green beetles.

There's plenty to see, with perched Berber villages Aremdt, Targa Imoula and Mzig within easy walking distance, and tea shops *en route*. For the ambitious, Toubkal itself stands waiting to be climbed, and for the culturally motivated the kasbah will also organise expeditions to neighbouring valleys, overnighting in Berber houses.

While you're here you will have a chance to witness the impact that tourism has on fairly primitive societies. People here are relatively poor, but nearly all of them now have satellite TV, with up to 200 channels. National television (of the sort which consists of government announcements and relies on transmitter masts) never made it up the valley, so now mountain people who still do all their cooking with hand-collected firewood are sitting open-jawed in front of the likes of MTV and late-night German sauciness. They're fascinated, but being good Muslims, they're also troubled by what they see.

Is this progress? Last time I was in these parts I was told a story about these mountain communities, about how many of the men, if they were French speaking, would go to work in France for the summer. Anyway, one year while they were away a well-known local singer had come on a tour, and someone had made a video of her performances which had then been shown to the menfolk on their return. Many recognised their wives in the audience, and divorces followed thick and fast; it seems that when the men were away, they expected their wives to maintain the house and the livestock, but otherwise stay indoors.

It seems harsh. But then, this is their culture, so who are we to say?

PRACTICALITIES

GETTING THERE

Easyjet

☏ *0905 821 0905; www.easyjet.com*

Flights from Gatwick to Marrakesh for upwards of £190 return.

The kasbah can arrange road transfers from Marrakesh at €80 for a car that seats four.

TOURIST INFORMATION

☏ *020 7437 0073; www.visitmorocco.org*

ACCOMMODATION

Kasbah du Toubkal $ $ $ $

Imlil

UK ☏ *01883 744392; www.kasbahdutoubkal.com*